To Reason Why

From Religion to Philosophy and Beyond

John Burnheim

DARLINGTON PRESS

First published by Darlington Press 2011
Darlington Press is an imprint of SYDNEY UNIVERSITY PRESS

Sydney University Press
Fisher Library F03, University of Sydney
NSW 2006 Australia
Email: sup.info@sydney.edu.au

National Library of Australia Cataloguing-in-Publication entry

Author: Burnheim, John.
Title: To reason why : from religion to philosophy and beyond /
          John Burnheim.
ISBN: 9781921364143 (pbk.)
Notes: Includes bibliographical references and index.
Subjects:
          Philosophers--Australia--Biography.
          Political science--Philosophy.
          Philosophy, Australian.
          Religion.
Dewey Number:
          109.2

Cover photo of the author by Robert Billington (1995).

Cover design by Miguel Yamin, the University Publishing Service

For those who do or die, there also have to be those who reason why.

André Brink

CONTENTS

INTRODUCTION

Brink described his own formula as 'glib' in the context of the struggle against apartheid, but still claimed 'there's a grain of truth in it'. As indeed there is, as I shall try to explain. But first let me introduce myself.

My defining image of myself belongs to late summer, 1944. I am standing in front of the magnificent sandstone building of St Patrick's College, Manly, the Alma Mater of the Australian priesthood, looking up along the great stretch of headlands and beaches between Sydney Heads and Broken Bay. It is late morning, the warm sun glints on the ocean swell as it rolls in to make surf along the beaches and fling spray on to the intervening cliffs. A tall, thin, erect figure, about to turn seventeen, with a long face, light brown hair, hooded blue eyes, a long nose and longer ears, I look preoccupied, serious but by no means lugubrious, in spite of my dress. I'm wearing a black serge cassock or soutane with a broad red sash, derived from the college's association with Propaganda, the central missionary college in Rome. It is said to symbolise the blood of martyrs. Australia still counts as a missionary country, subject to the papal congregation *De Propaganda Fide,* for the propagation of the faith, the origin of the modern word *propaganda.*

I have a powerful vision of my place in the scheme of things. The inexorable but beneficent power of the dazzling light in which sun, sea and land manifest the magnificent beauty of their creator evoke a sensation of trust in his will to transform the world. He is teaching us through the horrifying lessons of the war that is limping towards its conclusion how we must press forward on the ragged march that must ultimately lead back to him. I feel that the English-speaking peoples have a providential role, following their wartime mission against the forces of evil, in orienting the world towards an order based on justice, freedom and a genuine understanding of who we are. For all its imperfections, Australia is a striking example of what can be achieved in a very short time by people who can shake off the oppressive shackles of the past while preserving and developing their positive heritage. It has a special message for the times, but that message needs to be set in the context of the divine plan and draw on the power of God's grace. I am called to devote myself to convincing my countrymen of this necessity and to exploring its implications.

I shall try to explain how I came to be that person and what finally became of him. My first twenty-two years culminated in my ordination to the priesthood. My second twenty were spent as a priest trying to find in Catholic beliefs the remedy for the ills of the world. The third twenty were spent as a professional philosopher amid the turbulence that erupted in the late sixties, culminating in my publishing my own prescription for changing our political institutions. Now at the end of my fourth twenty years, in retirement, I attempt to sum it all up.

My story may be of some historical interest. I hope it will also interest people who are thinking about the great problems that face humankind in the twenty-first century. Not that those of us who devote themselves to thinking rather than doing are more likely to be right than anybody else. We too easily become obsessed with some partial vision of our situation. The history of philosophy can be read as a process of ricochets from one extreme to another. An old saying describes philosophers as 'making a living by taking in each other's washing.' A distinguished late nineteenth-century British philosopher, AC Bradley, once described philosophy as a matter of finding bad reasons for what we believe on instinct. We are very well aware that everybody is inclined to believe what it suits them to believe. So we tend to be sceptical about explaining people's changes of belief in terms of the validity of their reasons. What follows is the story of a life focused on a search for the right way of thinking about human life. I think that my choices have been guided by sound reasoning, but I offer my version of my choices not as an *apologia* but as an attempt to sharpen the issues involved. They are, I believe, not just religious and philosophical, but social and political, in particular a matter of how we can improve our collective decision procedures.

What individuals or groups choose may be a matter of their psychological needs. But what they *can* choose is a matter of what alternatives are on offer and what they can know about their advantages and disadvantages. The task of those who devote themselves to thinking is to clarify the choices that are available. When it comes to beliefs, whatever other desirable or undesirable features they may have, the strength of the evidence for or against them has to be relevant. Once our curiosity is aroused, we cannot be satisfied without evidence. We want to understand, to get it right. In complex matters the evidence is rarely completely conclusive, as the history of thinking in both science and philosophy shows. I believe that there is hardly ever conclusive evidence in favour of a philosophical position, but that some can be shown to be pretty certainly false. Still, it is not enough just to accept that a view is false. Especially in matters that have significant practical implications, we need to know not just that people got things wrong, but where exactly their beliefs were wrong and what, if anything, survives the needed corrections. Above all we need to see more clearly what constitutes a genuine step forward. That is the really hard part.

The story I have to tell may help in that task, precisely because it is about a past that is in many ways very different from the present. I see it as story of progress in a number of respects, for reasons I attempt to articulate. I may be wrong about that, but what I have to say may still be of use in providing readers with a view in which they can recognise clearly what they want to reject. That may enable them to clarify for themselves where they stand. More importantly, the assumptions with which I began my journey are not very widely held these days. I believed that religion, and, more generally, our conception of ourselves must rest on a set of completely objective truths, as strongly binding as those of mathematics. That assumption is deeply entrenched in Western culture, and its traces are still influential. So one often encounters the view that human life and concerns are insignificant because we are just tiny specks in the universe, as if our value was a matter of the objective physical facts about our size or our power rather than about what is distinctive of us, our knowledge, our loves and our moral worth.

It is often the case that in rejecting a way of looking at things we are too narrowly focused on the obvious differences between us and our opponents, neglecting certain assumptions that underpin, constrict and distort both positions. The atheist can be a prisoner of theism, confined to a purely negative position, as if all values collapsed when the theist account of them failed. Monism may consist simply in the refutation of dualism, without any account of the differences that support the dualist position. Similarly the materialist may be as limited as the idealist, the sceptic just as wrong as the dogmatist and so on. Hegel thought that out of conflicts in which one idea is just the antithesis of its opposite thinking one could arrive at a position that rises to a higher level, getting beyond the assumptions that underpinned the conflict. Whether that is generally possible in the way he suggested, I very much doubt. But it is always worth trying. I hope to tell this story in a way that may bring into question some elusive assumptions that still need to be challenged if we are to get beyond many of the apparently sterile conflicts that continue to shackle our thinking. More positively I have some practical suggestions about organising our ways of making decisions in the light of new perspectives.

Some of what follows, the heart of it in fact, discusses the work of professional philosophers. I hope I have succeeded in making that work intelligible to readers with no previous acquaintance with it. I don't think that is too difficult. Obviously, what follows is simplified, and may well be misleading. One cannot guard against the myriad possibilities of misunderstanding, but if the reader does not read too much into what my words say, it should not be too difficult to understand. What is much harder to convey is why anybody should be concerned about such theoretical problems. Like most professional philosophers I think that problems of the sort we discuss often underlie people's beliefs and attitudes, and that making them explicit can sometimes help people make better judgments about their lives. Philosophy is supposed to be the love of wisdom. Whatever about its success in getting things right, its getting them wrong can be very dangerous. Even a proposition that is clearly true can be misleading if it is taken as the whole truth about a certain matter. Once we go beyond particular facts, which are mostly trivial, truth claims are always contestable. But they can still have drastic practical consequences, notoriously so in matters of religion, morality or politics. Because truth demands assent it brings the temptation to enforce acceptance of it in practice where the consequences of failing to heed it seem important. Similarly, error may seem to require forcible correction. The analogy with measures to control disease and protect public health is always at hand.

The most dangerous word philosophers can use is 'only'. Everybody knows that it is possible to write an account of an historical event that contains only true sentences but is quite wrong if it is taken as an adequate account of what happened. On the other hand, no account can ever be completely adequate in every respect. In the physical sciences it may perhaps be different. Certainly physicists aspire to a complete theory of the fundamental constituents of the universe. I think that philosophy is more like history than physics. The great strength of physics is that it can identify and quantify the factors with which it deals and interrelate them by precise mathematical formulae. Verbal descriptions in ordinary language or even in technical terms can only sit pretty loosely on the core procedures with which physics works. That is why popular expositions of physics are so often dubious, even where the authors are competent physicists. But physics, in being precise, abstracts from many aspects of things that we can grasp only in terms of much vaguer concepts, which can compensate to some extent by having a much richer content.

It is impoverishing and dangerous to ignore ambitious truth claims simply because they are vague. Vagueness is indeed dangerous. It makes it easy to conceal falsity, to confuse issues and to claim undue significance. That many people attach great importance to a belief may be simply that they are confused, mistaken, manipulated by scaremongers or victims of wishful thinking. But we have to start with what is vague and avoid the temptation of dogmatic prescriptions for a false precision that simply excises much that is important. Many people's philosophical problems appear intractable because of imposing impossible requirements on what they will accept as a solution. As Wittgenstein put it, 'to show the fly the way out of the fly-bottle' in such cases is a matter of bringing it to see just how the bottle gives the illusion of being completely enveloping. The great danger for philosophers is concentrating on one type of example to the exclusion of others that are equally relevant.

There is also a fundamental difference between the role ascribed to claims of complete theoretical adequacy in physics and in philosophy. In physics it has frequently been possible to discover previously unknown entities by showing definitively that existing theory cannot account for certain phenomena. Physics is always open to recognising entirely new entities and finding new kinds of theories to account for them, precisely because there is no way of accounting for them in existing theories. In philosophy, however, the usual role of claims to theoretical adequacy is the opposite of this. Philosophers typically strive to marginalise, explain away or ignore what their theories cannot account for, dismissing it as illusory or irrelevant, just because they want to maintain that their account is the whole truth of the matter. What follows may illustrate how dangerous and unwarranted claims of complete adequacy or exclusive truth are in philosophy, as in all the humanities and social sciences. But first a sketch of the background.

1

Growing Up in the Thirties

In the mid twentieth century Australian nuclear families built walls around themselves. One's identity tended to be determined principally by family upbringing to an extent that is hard to imagine today amid the swarming influences of TV, mobile phones and the internet, the decline in the demands of respectability and the relaxation of parental discipline. The standards that Australian middle-class and 'solid' working-class parents accepted and enforced in the first half of the twentieth century were substantially those of Victorian Britain, only slightly revised in favour of sentiment rather than discipline and unpretentiousness rather than claims to social standing.

My parents exemplified the paradoxical combination of an extreme subservience to convention and a firm insistence that you should not be concerned about what others thought or said about you. All that mattered was what one believed was right and proper. Their conception of morality unknowingly followed Adam Smith in his *Theory of Moral Sentiments*. Faced with dubious or conflicting demands one appeals from them to what one believes the impartial observer would approve. But, having appealed to the authority of that construct, one can justify one's own behaviour only by applying its verdicts to oneself. Morality is internalised in the inexorable dialectic of the need for self-approval. It was called obeying one's own conscience. Morality was raised above mere convention or mere sentiment. It was refined, explicated and developed in submitting the demands of feeling and fashion to those of consistency and impartiality.

Of course, not everybody feels the need for self-justification. Some people manage to convince themselves that they can ignore all questions of moral consistency and reject demands for impartiality as chimerical and ridiculously restrictive. They are not necessarily frivolous. They may follow certain versions of Nietzsche or Ayn Rand that exalt the liberty of the strong as the great creative force that is constantly threatened by the negativity and mediocrity of popular morality. I shall have something to say about such views later on.

I thoroughly internalised the view, which was to stay with me for the rest of my life, that one's conscience is the most important element in one's identity. It was not incompatible with accepting the view that morality was a matter of divine commandments, since these needed to be interpreted in detail and applied conscientiously to particular instances and the need for self-approval could be understood as a derivative of the need for divine approval. Nevertheless, for a strict Catholic such an interpretation left an unresolved tension in practice between obedience to the moral prescriptions of the church and following one's own conscience where they seemed to conflict. More fundamentally, just as it was impossible to assent rationally to what one saw as false, it seemed impossible to assent conscientiously to prescriptions one saw as morally wrong. Of course, given that the church was infallible, and that nobody's personal judgment was incorrigible, such conflict could only show that one had made a mistake, probably a culpable mistake, in the particular instance. Radical conflict emerged only when conscience and authority disagreed systematically in what they saw to be morally relevant.

The great danger in making self-approval the motive force in morality is that of 'taking yourself too seriously', shutting off the great range of other relationships and interactions and ambitions that make life richly varied and surprising. To make moral seriousness central to one's identity is to invite the derision of those who see morality as the refuge of those who are neither clever enough nor strong enough to seize the opportunities that life offers to enterprise and imagination. In Australia even the most respectable, such as my parents, were sensitive to such ridicule and felt somewhat vulnerable in their self-approval. They were torn between wanting to live up to their ideals and wanting to disclaim any pretensions to moral superiority over the less serious. Morality tended to be split into two disparate areas, a matter of the individual's personal values and feelings on the one hand and of conventional prohibitions and obligations on the other.

This dichotomy in turn affected their religious life. It was assumed that everybody had a religious affiliation to some ecclesiastical organisation and that the churches were entitled to a certain respect. On the other hand, one's religion was a private domain, a matter of pious feelings. Religious practice in this context tended to be personal and dutiful, at best consoling, never joyous or triumphant or liberating. The liturgy involved a lot of individuals attending mass without ever expressing any deeper relation to each other than that of happening to be doing the same thing in the same place at the same time. The dominant image of counter-reformation Catholicism, the son of God dying in agony on the cross under the weight of our sins, was softened only by that of Mary, his mother who was ever ready to intercede for us, to mitigate our miseries, appealing from divine justice to divine mercy. In this perspective one's relation to the redeemer was a very personal and private matter.

In one of the great theological revolutions, hidden behind the vague formulae of creedal continuity, the redemption was no longer demanded by the inexorable demands of divine justice requiring infinite reparation for the infinite insult that the smallest sin offered to the divine majesty. Instead it showed the depth of God's love for each and every one of us that he would go to extreme lengths to show us the way to eternal bliss. The objective guilt of offending the divine majesty was supplanted by the subjective guilt of not returning the divine love as it deserved. The change was obviously a matter of the culture of democratisation. Offences against the majesty of monarchs were no longer all that important. The church adapted to change easily enough when its authority was not threatened. In either case, the emphasis on sin as a matter of divine law was unhealthy and distracted from a clear focus on what it was about an action that made it morally wrong and consequently forbidden.

A more virile strand in Australian Catholic tradition sought to counter the puritanism and sentimentality into which the religion of suffering so easily descended by endorsing wholeheartedly the great Australian enthusiasm for the 'innocent pleasures' of sport, sun and surf. The attitude that the comfortable golf-playing clergy seemed to encourage was that Jesus Christ had paid the price of our sins, displaying the depth of God's love for us. It was a gratuitous gesture. We did not have to pay again. Assured of God's love we could be confident that he would welcome us into heaven, after a negotiable period of cleaning up in purgatory, if he could possibly do so within the rules. We must avoid stretching his forgiveness too far. As a religion for a commercialised democratic society it was a comfortable, reasonable compromise. In this respect it was not very different from establishment Protestantism. Religion had come a long way since the days when it was almost unanimously assumed that all the children of Adam and Eve were condemned to eternal damnation and only a chosen few could be saved. Religion was consoling rather than threatening. Losing one's faith was a tragedy, not a liberation.

Barney

My parents belonged to the stricter end of the spectrum that this compromising religious practice allowed. My father, Bernard Gorman Burnheim, born in 1891, known as Barney, was one of the youngest of the thirteen children sired by his father, a lamplighter in

18

Balmain, then populated by miners and wharf-labourers. My grand-father was born on the Omeo goldfields in Victoria to an illiterate immigrant of unknown origins who arrived in Sydney in the early 1840s. Barney received a basic education under the tough regime of the Irish Christian Brothers until he left school at the age of twelve. He took a job looking after the horses of an itinerant peddler who roamed the south coast of New South Wales selling sheet music and spectacles from his caravan. Barney earned enough money to pay for a course in the not yet feminised skills of shorthand and typing and to lay-by clothes suitable to office work.

As a child he had contracted polio, which left him with a shrivelled left leg. With specially made boots, he walked confidently and vigorously, but participation in most of the sports he loved was closed to him. One that was available was body surfing. In middle age he still went to the beach before work most mornings in summer. He was a handsome man with a clear, firm voice and a very presentable and manly manner. The family background was wholly Irish, nobody recalling the origins of the German name. During the Great War it was asserted to be Swiss. One of Barney's brothers anglicised it to Burnham. In any case, all his able-bodied brothers enlisted to fight for King and country.

He soon found his lifetime employment in the head office of Winchcombe Carson, one of the great 'wool firms' that were central to the economy when Australia 'rode on the sheep's back', supplying most of the world trade in wool when wool was indispensible for keeping everybody warm in winter and presentably tailored in every season. He rose to become manager of the stock and property division of the firm, claiming the unique distinction of having personally sold over a million head of stock, sheep and cattle, in a single year, without leaving his Sydney office.

The network through which this trading was negotiated depended entirely on Barney's reputation for knowledge and integrity. Buyers would accept his account of the condition of sheep he had never seen, based on his knowledge of their origins and their grazier's reliability. Sellers would accept his judgment of the market and his assurance that they would be paid promptly. The firm would advance finance for the deal on his assurance that it would be covered by the proceeds of the buyer's next wool clip. The deal would be sealed over the phone and only later confirmed in writing. Unfortunately he was on salary rather than a commission. The Burnheims lived comfortably, but frugally through the Great Depression.

Like so many self-made men he was very conservative in his social and political opinions, though he tended to keep them to himself. In the circles in which he moved talk of politics or religion, indeed of anything other than business or sport, was taboo. At home children and women were deemed not to be capable of understanding matters of public import, something that annoyed my mother from time to time. He and mother treated each other with respect and consideration, rather than affection, though they tended to bicker tediously about trifles. Barney was conventionally, though very seriously, if reticently, pious. 'A devout Catholic.' Although he and Kate had only three children, as opposed to their parents' dozens, that was no doubt ensured in ways that met with the approval of the church.

Kate

Kate Radnedge and Barney Burnheim were in every way suited to each other. Their relationship rested on thorough mutual understanding, shared values and mutual trust. A big, handsome woman with strong features and presence, she was, rather oddly, known from childhood as 'Tot'. Though dogmatic in tone and inclined to attribute unflattering motives to others, she was insistent on the importance of tolerance. At the same time as she drilled into her children the importance of following their own conscience, whatever others might think, she displayed a respect for authority that was reminiscent of a time when forms of address such as 'your reverence' or 'your worship' were supposed to express the appropriate attitude to the office bearers who claimed them. The obverse of this respect was her disgust when they failed to meet her standards.

Born in 1897, Kate was one of the younger daughters of a prosperous rural family, Australian for several generations, but of wholly English stock. Brought up Anglican, she converted to Catholicism at marriage, apparently without causing surprise or misgiving in her family. She had only an elementary education, never worked outside the home, and her knowledge of the world was very limited. Like Barney, she never read a book and saw no point in book learning. Molong, near which she grew up, was a prosperous town, just big enough and far enough from nearby Orange to sustain a social life with some pretensions to style and refinement, a world of tennis clubs, proper dances and picnic races that reflected the prosperity of the graziers with largish holdings, who were, for historical reasons, called 'squatters'. After the Great War many of these holdings were broken up to provide farms of precarious viability for returned soldiers and little of the 'squattocracy' survived.

The 1914–18 war was central to Kate's experience of life. In her late teens all her brothers enlisted in the AIF and served overseas. Jack, her favourite, was killed and several others severely wounded. She threw herself into raising money for the Red Cross, knitting socks for soldiers and other suitable efforts in support of the boys at the front. After the war and the death of her father Kate's mother sold the family property and took the girls to live in Manly, just around the corner from the house that was to be hers from the eve of the Second World War until the year before her death, fifty-eight years later. Barney happened also to be living in Manly at the time. They married in 1925 after he had bought a smallish new house in the developing suburb of Balgowlah, where they lived until 1939. I was born in 1927, followed by Margaret (Meg) two years later and Phillip three years after that. The family led a very domestic life, varied only by visits to and from relatives and the occasional trip to the beach.

There was no car, but the tram ran past the end of the street, linking with the ferry at Manly wharf.

There were no 'modern conveniences', 'mod cons' in the real estate jargon, no internal toilet or hot water on tap, much less a refrigerator or washing machine. The one extravagance was a radio, at a time when such apparatus was very expensive, unreliable and poorly served by transmitting stations. These became adequate only in the early to mid thirties, when the technology improved dramatically and government licence fees and commercial advertising began to provide substantial funding. The other source of entertainment was the 'picture theatre', at least one in every suburb, including one just around the corner from the Burnheim home. While their parents went to 'the pictures' infrequently (baby-sitters had not been invented), the young Burnheims, like most children, packed into the cinemas on Saturday afternoon for special children's programs, learning to identify the 'goodies', the manly white males, who naturally always won in the end. It was not a good social, cultural or political education.

School

From the age of six I caught the tram on my own down to Manly to the Christian Brothers College (CBC). Children in those days enjoyed much greater freedom of movement unsupervised than their successors today, in recreation as well as necessary travel. To be accompanied to school or sport would have been a fatal blow to one's standing in the eyes of one's peers. Although there was known to be some risk of encounters with paedophiles, the dangers were regarded very differently from today. Paedophiles were seen as pathetic by adults and the object of sniggering contempt by the young. It was assumed that a healthy child would quickly get over any encounter with such a pervert. Although some scoutmasters were often suspected of unhealthy interests, few parents hesitated to enrol their boys in the scouts. Even at CBC some of the brothers were the targets of insinuations by students who were fascinated by the arcana of sex. In any case, the unanimous attitude of adults was that such incidents as did occur should be hushed up. As always, that meant that the victims never got to explain how they were affected and the damage done to them was not appreciated. People did not want to know.

As in most societies, various juvenile subcultures had their own structures of affiliation, language, rules and sanctions that were carefully concealed from adults. In my environment these identifications were relatively weak compared to those of the closely regulated and scrutinised structures of the family. There could be no doubt about the sincerity of my parents' concern for their children's wellbeing and very little about the wisdom of their judgments about what was good for them. Being a good child was neither difficult nor unrewarding. My need to construct an individual identity for myself took the path, not of revolt against parental restrictions on my behaviour, but of reaching out to a world that for them hardly existed, the limitless reaches of knowledge. I became an insatiable reader. The school had no library, and home provided only an incomplete set of the novels of Dickens and a cheap encyclopaedia, both of them rewards for subscriptions to newspapers or magazines. The main contribution to a broader education was a subscription to the *National Geographic*. But I discovered the local public library and mined it randomly but persistently.

In 1938, as I turned eleven, we celebrated the 150th anniversary of the foundation of Australia. It was not so long ago. My grandparents may well have known people who arrived on the First Fleet. People who were unequivocally Australian still spoke of a trip to Britain as 'going home'. At the same time, there was a strong feeling that Australia had arrived at maturity. We had grown beyond the world of Henry Lawson and the crude nationalism of *The Bulletin*. The iconography of the sesquicentenary was streamlined, urban and forward-looking. A token of the future was the inauguration of a regular flying boat service between Australia and the United Kingdom. It took less than two weeks as against the ocean liner's five. It was a luxury for the very rich, particularly because the planes could fly only by day, and luxury hotels were provided each night. The big thing for ordinary mortals was that airmail made exchanging letters with the other side of the world so much faster. One could now speak to people overseas by telephone and short-wave radios pulled in transmissions from all over the world. New technology was going to dominate our future in ways that we could hardly envisage.

In the background there were a few murmurs from the people we had displaced, which we were assured we need not be too concerned about. They were a dying race, doomed to be absorbed pretty rapidly into the white community. So we could admire pictures of proud hunters and wonder at how they survived without agriculture or domestic animals in such an unforgiving climate, without any thought that they might have a future as a people. Australia was aggressively white, more so than Britain itself! There was no place in this country for racial minorities of any sort. I'm afraid I grew up as unthinkingly racist as most of my contemporaries.

An Introduction to Philosophy

The seeds of my lifelong involvement with philosophy were sown in the course of the religious instruction that was central to Catholic education in those days. At thirteen I was introduced to Archbishop Sheehan's *Apologetics,* which outlined the classical arguments for the existence of God, the historical evidence for the miracles and claims of Jesus and the argument that he committed his authority on earth to St Peter and his successors as bishop of Rome. The implicit message was that none of these foundational beliefs could be taken for granted or assumed to be self-evident. Of course, those who were fortunate enough to have the gift of faith, the inner conviction of a life with God in the community of the church, had no more need to worry about the theoretical presuppositions of that faith than to worry about the physics of the sun that sustained their physical lives. Nevertheless, understanding was important, both for its intrinsic value as truth and its role in showing unbelievers that there were sound objective grounds for believing. It was not just a matter of personal feelings or opinions, as most people assumed. What mattered was to ground one's life on what was objectively true. As Catholic apologists put it to heretics of all sorts, 'you worship God in your way, but we worship him in his'.

Taking such questions seriously was implicitly to challenge the conformist consensus that society lived by tradition. Morality was a matter of 'the demands of society', sanctified by religion as the recognised custodian of 'spiritual values' in an otherwise materialistic world. Exclusive claims to religious truth were at best socially irrelevant and at worst politically sectarian. The ruling political ideology was a version of the British imperialist tradition that was given definitive expression in the myth of the Anzacs with their distinctively irreverent but still unquestioning devotion to 'the Empire on which the sun never sets' and its mission of bringing civilisation to the rest of the world. At the beginning of every cinema performance we all stood in silence for 'God save the King'. In the common experience of life seen in this light the old distrust of Catholics and Protestants for each other lost its force. The ecumenical movement was a long way off, but tolerance ruled. People expected each other to be loyal to their own church in strictly religious, largely personal, matters, but this was of little political or social significance. Australian Catholics no longer identified with Irish nationalism, stressing the distinctiveness of their Australian identity.

A World in Turmoil

I share birthdays with Adolph Hitler, although I was unaware of the fact when Hitler began to take an important role in my development. What came to dominate my view of life was the sense that there was something wrong with the whole structure of the secular world. My reading soon revealed that all over the world there were powerful, conflicting forces striving to change radically the ways in which public affairs, and indeed the everyday lives of people, were organised. The easy assumption that everything would be all right if only individuals were less sinful could hardly be sustained any longer. What was wrong was not just a matter of the sins of individuals. Indeed even the Pope had issued an encyclical that acknowledged that there must be a Christian response to the demand for a solution to the systemic problems that the Great War and the Great Depression had forced all thinking people to acknowledge. This was especially important because the main contenders in the arena, communism and fascism, were entirely unacceptable from a Christian point of view.

My interest in the ideological conflicts of the time was precocious, naive and idiosyncratic. In 1939 I read somewhere that Hitler boasted that he had understood the German problem since the age of thirteen. I considered that I understood the problem, and I was only twelve! What is certain is that we were not talking about the same thing. I am not sure where I derived my understanding of the situation in Europe. I remember the journalism of Emery Barcs, who arrived from Hungary as a refugee in 1938 and spoke with authority on what was happening in central Europe. At some stage in 1938 I read *The House that Hitler Built* by Stephen Roberts, professor of history at Sydney University, known to schoolboys as the author of the prescribed text on modern history. Roberts left no doubt about Hitler's ambitions. Not everything was clear-cut. The one thing that was never questioned was that the British Empire was the great force for good in the world, the greatest and noblest empire the world had ever seen. On the other hand, the Spanish Civil War was confusing. The Republican government was the legitimate authority, but there seemed to be some substance in the claim that it had been taken over by communists, who persecuted the church.

In Australia there was no avowedly fascist organisation and the Communist Party remained a small sect, though vocal and well organised. But it was clear that large sections of the population were ready to embrace one or the other extreme if it came to crisis. I was appalled to hear a friend of my father returning from Germany proclaim that Hitler was doing a wonderful job of putting the Jews in their place. Mussolini was admired for getting the trains to run on time. Democratic politicians were hopeless, incompetent and venal, and rule by popular opinion absurd. What the country needed was a dictator who would clean up the mess and provide real leadership. Behind the mess, of course, were the Jews, who were flooding into the country compounding its subservience to international finance, sucking its lifeblood.

On the other hand, my cousin, Harry Radnedge, also from a pious Catholic family, and about to embark on a lifelong career in the police force, was converted to communism by Dean Hewlett Johnson's *The Socialist Sixth of the World* (1939). A great many people were prepared to grant that in principle communism was the ideal form of social organisation, while remaining very sceptical about its achievability in practice. They felt a certain sympathy with and admiration for the great Soviet 'experiment', while remaining unconvinced that it was succeeding and largely ignorant of its horrors. Many trade union activists, soured by unemployment, were prepared to grant that what was needed was a revolution that would inevitably lead to bloodshed as the capitalist strove violently to repress it. But few saw any prospect of mobilising the politically comatose local proletariat to act. Protest was routinely dismissed as the work of professional malcontents and 'stirrers' who could be dismissed without any consideration of what they were saying.

The war put an end to the depression, leading many to reflect that there was never a problem in mobilising resources for war, but not for peace. It also defined Nazism and fascism as the enemy, exposed the communists as opportunistic and unreliable allies, and glorified democracy as the banner under which we fought. Vague promises that the mistakes of the past that had led to war would never be repeated catered to people's need to believe that the slaughter was not destined to be as futile as that in the First World War, which was still vivid in the memories of many people who survived it. Conventional patriotism reigned unchallenged.

In 1942, as the war came close to Australia, Meg, Phil and I were sent to boarding school in Katoomba in the Blue Mountains. It was my matriculation year, and the change was damaging academically. St Bernard's was just opening, and quite unprepared to cater for Leaving Certificate students, but the family home was near the forts on North Head that guarded the entrance to Sydney Harbour and were considered a prime target for an invading force. Manly beach was no longer devoted to surfing, but festooned with barbed wire and fortifications. Several Japanese midget submarines did succeed in penetrating the defences of the harbour and came near to causing serious damage.

Against the background of these events my precocious concern about the state of the world took a specifically religious focus. I thought that the answer to the problems that beset us had to lie in the redemptive mission of the son of God, embodied in the Catholic Church. So I decided that I was called to become a priest, bringing to the world the enlightenment of his message and the power of his grace.

2

Redeeming the Time: A Clerical Education[1]

In 1943, having completed my schooling at the age of fifteen, I entered the seminary, St Columba's College, at Springwood, also in the Blue Mountains, to begin the seven years of study required of candidates for the priesthood. After a year at Springwood I progressed to the imposing St Patrick's College at Manly, only a block away from home. The pattern of life in these institutions has been described by Tom Keneally in the novels, *The Place at Whitton* and *Three Cheers for the Paraclete,* by Christopher Geraghty in the memoirs, *The Priest Factory* and *Cassocks in the Wilderness,* and by Paul Crittenden in his memoirs, *Changing Orders.* There is no point in attempting more here. The pictures painted by Keneally and Geraghty are grim. Crittenden is kinder. It was a monastic regime, in which every minute of the day was allocated to a prescribed activity. No food or drink was allowed other than what the college provided. No smoking, no phones or radios, no newspapers or magazines, and so on. In the college one wore a cassock at all times, except for sport, and outside a black suit, black tie and felt hat. Students were allowed

---

1 The phrase 'redeeming the time' occurs in most of the older translations of Ephesians 5.16 and Colossians 4.5. It was taken to refer to the role of Christians in changing the world, but modern commentators and translators tell us that Paul was merely admonishing his followers to use their time well, as if they were retrieving it or buying it back from the forces of evil. The phrase provided the title for a book by Jacques Maritain in its English translation, which influenced me strongly in my Thomist days.

to leave the college grounds only on rare occasions, though they were allowed an annual vacation at home, subject to certain restrictions, under the supervision of their parish priest. While many found the regime an irksome imposition to be survived as a protracted initiation, a test of one's suitability for ordination, others, including me, adapted to it more easily.

It was a great help to be fairly self-sufficient, to have some real interests that could be pursued within the rules and were shared by some of one's colleagues. I was fortunate in having a weak sex appetite. Perhaps I had been inoculated to an extent by having spent so much of my childhood at the beach among scantily clad women. I began to masturbate, and then only infrequently, well into my twenties, after ordination. I had no experience of sexual intercourse until twenty years later, after I left the church. The downside of my retarded development was a lack of spontaneous responsiveness to other people. Even my friends often felt I was aloof, in spite of my efforts to draw closer to them. It did not help that I was younger and less experienced than any of my classmates, many of whom were 'late vocations', for whom I was just a naive kid. I was very unassertive and hopeless at most sports, especially team sports. My favourite recreation was surfing, which was usually a solitary occupation. On the other hand, my low sex drive was probably what spared me the tormented conviction, so common among all strands of Christian spirituality, of being an abject sinner, totally corrupted by the world, the flesh and the devil. I thought of myself as far from perfect, but living in a state in which I could rely on God's grace, dispensed through the sacraments, to keep on improving my performance, as long as I kept on practising the virtues and suppressing 'sinful thoughts' or undue attention to the sexual aspects of physical beauty.

My orientation was in fact thoroughly positive. I was not so much concerned with avoiding sin; I wanted to become a saint. I would never have described my ambition in those terms, but that was what it amounted to. What I would have said was that I wanted to do what

God wanted of me, and to do it as well as possible. That was the only sustainable answer to what one should do with one's life. That was how we were designed to live. I had come to believe that what God wanted of me was to be a Catholic priest, and that meant reliving in a special way the mission of Jesus Christ himself, becoming, as the exhortations put it, 'another Christ'. Among the numerous forms of ministry available within the priesthood, I seemed to be called particularly to the task of articulating and presenting the message of the church in a way that was relevant to the problems of the middle of the twentieth century.

The scope of the problems facing humanity as a whole was in every respect unprecedented. For the first time every person on the planet was entangled inescapably in the same web of economic, political and cultural interactions. Modern communications were annihilating distance, modern technology was transforming our work, our relations to nature and our control over our bodies. Education was spreading literacy and scientific thinking across all cultural differences. Mere traditionalism was everywhere unsustainable. If one believed in divine providence and the revelation brought by the son of God to save all mankind, one could hardly fail to see that this extraordinary explosion of the scale of the workings of the world must be matched by an equally portentous change in the mission of the church through which God conveyed his message to the world. The church could no longer look back to its golden age in medieval Europe for the model on which to conduct its role in the modern world. It must face problems that posed themselves in entirely new terms. It must take the full measure of its global mission for the first time, rise above a narrowly Europe-centred perspective and speak to a scientific and critical age in a language that it could understand.

I had enormous confidence in the vision I mentioned earlier as my defining self-image. It would continue to sustain me through to my early forties. At the same time I was aware that it was my perspective, not some God's eye view. Others were equally seized by very different visions even though grounded in the same sources, scripture and Christian tradition. For me the fact that the second person of the trinity had taken a fully human identity was proof that humanity could express the divine and was ultimately destined to do so. The sufferings of the son of God on the cross were real, but just the prelude to the resurrection, not just the survival of the soul, but the resurrection of the body, the fulfilment of human history.

No doubt my affinity with this optimistic vision was grounded in my experience of life. I never wanted for anything. My parents assured me of all the material and spiritual support I needed. I never had to fight or even to compete for anything. Such success as I valued came from doing what I was required to do and encouraged to do. I suffered no great inner conflicts, no dark night of the soul.

A contrary vision was possible, and many shared it. The cosmos was torn in an endless struggle between good and evil, between God and the world, the flesh and the devil. That conflict that was destined to end in the triumph of good, not in this world, but in the next. Christ rose from the dead and made a few appearances to his disciples, but he did not continue to live among them. On the contrary he promised to take them out of this world when it was finally condemned. Evil would be defeated, but not destroyed, burned alive for all eternity in hell. Such a vision might well seem more authentic to those who took the full measure of the times.

Each vision teetered on the brink of heresy, in the first case a sort of pantheism, breaking down the gulf between the human and the divine, in the second a Manicheism that made the devil as primordial as the godhead. The simplistic visions that individuals could grasp were inevitably inadequate to the divine order. The full truth belonged to the collective mind of the church, whose task it was to interpret the relevance of that truth to successive generations in the light of the needs of the time.

I had no doubt that the church would be guided by providence towards the answers to those problems, but it was hampered by the tendency to present those answers in terms of facile dichotomies, anachronistic imagery, and specious pointscoring. What mattered was not to show that *we* were right, which we did not deserve, but to bring people to the Truth, in spite of our faulty presentation of it. For example, an indiscriminate hostility to the modern world was validated by dubious constructs of the age of faith. Getting beyond this negativity involved many dimensions, but the official voice of the church insisted that one key to a renewed theological and cultural approach to the modern world lay in the works of the great medieval thinker-saint Thomas Aquinas. Thomism represented the fullest articulation of the great vision in which all things proceeded from God and ultimately returned to him. It expressed the unity of faith and reason that had subsequently been lost in the confusion of subsequent thinking. I plunged into the task of mastering that thought with a view to understanding our modern predicament.

Thomism: A Fight Against Error or a Search for Understanding?

Many took this to mean that the task in hand was to formulate more rigorously the characteristic theses of the Thomist synthesis and rebut the host of opposing positions that had emerged since the thirteenth century. So the typical textbooks used in theological and philosophical courses in seminaries began by listing errors to be refuted and proceeding to reject them as incompatible with the truth for which the text provided a conclusive proof. Within the bounds of this rigid orthodoxy there were significant theoretical differences on matters of technical detail, but any suggestion that there might be questions to which the tradition had no answer or answers that might be questionable was rigorously excluded.

The spirit in which St Thomas presented his thoughts was very different. Typically every topic was presented as a question to which the answer could not be assumed to be known in advance. The initial approach to it listed a variety of reasons why opposite answers might seem plausible. The arguments of Maimonides the Jew and Avicenna and Averroes, the great Muslim thinkers, were treated as worthy of careful consideration alongside those of Augustine and Origen. After presenting the arguments for his own position Aquinas returned to a further analysis of the other positions, typically conceding that there was some point in their argument, but that it relied on a failure to make some relevant distinction.

Such a mode of presentation had its limitations. It could easily degenerate into a process where the questions were rigged and the saving distinctions were specious. It also left unclear just what were the principles on which the author's own position rested. Very often propositions and distinctions were invoked in the course of answering various questions in different contexts without ever being explained explicitly in their own right. So there was ample scope for rival schools to construct different frameworks offering different explications of the underlying concepts and principles of Thomism. Inward-looking controversies between such schools engaged very much more attention than the questions raised by modern thought.

Although I felt dissatisfied with this situation, I was inevitably confined within it. I had no access to any postmedieval philosophy apart from a few inadequate accounts in approved histories of philosophy. Most of the relevant original texts were on the *Index of Prohibited Books* and were in any case unavailable in the seminary library. I had no contact with anybody who had an interest in conceptual questions beyond the confines of scholasticism. In philosophy I read only Aquinas and some of his commentators until I came across the exciting work of Jacques Maritain, a new French lay voice who addressed contemporary concerns in the light of a fresh approach to Aquinas. I found new hope, as we shall see.

My interests did not meet with the approval of my superiors in the seminary. They were very distrustful of the impulse to independent thinking. The root source of most error was intellectual pride, the urge to put one's own judgment above that of everybody else. Pride was the worst of all sins, the sin of Lucifer himself, and intellectual pride was the source of all error, the basic spiritual evil, compared to which sins of the flesh were relatively innocuous. I was warned that I read too much, even among the innocent tomes that seminarians were permitted to read. One should concentrate on mastering the approved texts and on striving to discover the wisdom they encapsulated.

Awful as it sounds today, this regime was only an extreme instance of much educational practice at the time, especially in Australia. A great deal of professional education was devoted to rote learning of facts and terminology without any critical understanding. Much general education continued to be dominated by 'a Classical education' that cultivated facility in Latin and Greek and the capacity to enliven one's utterances with hackneyed Latin tags. At Sydney University the philosophical radical John Anderson dictated his lectures to students who were expected to take them down and regurgitate them in the examinations.

Pride and Prejudices

From their own point of view the seminary authorities were completely right. In their view truth is eternal, brought to us definitively in the incarnation, transmitted infallibly through the tradition of the church. To hanker for novelty, to set oneself up as a critic of traditional approaches was to pit one's own judgment against the consensus of the custodians of traditional wisdom. That in itself was intellectual pride, especially in a youngster who had not yet gone through a thorough training in traditional practices. The brash intellectual chasing after novelties was the antithesis of the genuine scholar treasuring and transmitting the rich heritage of tradition.

The modesty this view prized was powerfully reinforced by traditional spirituality. In Catholic tradition, as in the great spiritual traditions of Asia, the central aim of spiritual life was the cleansing of the soul from all impurity of motivation. That could never be achieved by relying on one's own judgment. One must submit humbly to the guidance of those who have been through the process, who can show the way step by step. Attempting to achieve any deep purification by unaided self-scrutiny locked one in to one's own myopic and defective perceptions. Modern individualism bridled at the necessity of spiritual asceticism, but the truth was that the only unqualified good was holiness, being united in mind, affect and will with the divine.

With some misgivings and a lot of backsliding, I took to heart what my superiors enjoined. In practice it was not harsh, especially on one who by temperament was relatively self-sufficient. Humility required that one did not pretend to tastes or capacities or achievements that were superior to those of one's colleagues. Being 'singular' was dangerous, as were cliques or 'particular friendships'. The regime enjoined a conformity that was very congenial to the pervasive distrust of intellectual, aesthetic or moral pretensions throughout Australian life.

About the only mundane interest that I shared with many of my colleagues was a fascination with cars, a part of my lifelong interest in architecture, design and engineering. Even as a child I loved taking toys to pieces to find out how they worked. When my parents urged me to try other options before committing myself to the priesthood, the recognised profession that attracted me was architecture. Design problems and the way mechanical things worked always fascinated me. I loved repairing things, or even just taking them to pieces and reassembling them. More profoundly, my early experience of the sea and the mountains, with their grand vistas and awesome power, formed the basis of an almost mystical sense of the wonders of nature. I have always had the good fortune to live in surroundings that provided nourishment for that feeling. As soon as I could in later life I took up sailing and found a deep satisfaction in what was described as 'the poetry of motion', especially in solo sailing, where the sailor, the boat, the wind and the sea came together in a continually changing harmony.

A Conformist Context

What the seminaries were designed to produce were shepherds of the flock, pastors, administering sacramental nourishment to the faithful, chasing up the lost sheep and providing reliable guidance about the way to heaven. What mattered was the salvation of souls. The priest, and in a measure the pious lay person had to 'be in the world, but not of the world'. Ultimately, nothing in this world mattered, except in its bearing on the life to come. The pains and sorrows of life were 'crosses we have to bear', tests 'sent to try us', opportunities to draw nearer to the crucified Christ. Concerns about the health of civil society, about abolishing injustice rather than accepting it as the way of the world, about excellence and beauty, were all very well up to a point, but they were all secondary considerations and in any case doomed to failure in a world thoroughly vitiated by sin.

In historical perspective this regime could be represented as a tradition going back to the Jesus of the gospel, the Jesus who showed an ambivalent attitude to the ordinary concerns of mundane living, replenishing the wine at the marriage feast of Cana, healing the sick, comforting the afflicted, but also warning that even the most sacred duties to parents and kin must be put aside if they stood in the way of following the path to salvation. Socially and politically the compromise that the church reached with secular society harked back to Jesus' dictum about rendering to Caesar what is his and to God what is God's. Almost every aspect of public life belonged to Caesar. God's part was largely private.

That compromise destroyed any possibility of religion finding adequate expression in social life. That was just as well, since the only way that the hierarchy could envisage such an expression was in terms of the state subjecting itself to the church. In social practice religion was reduced to tribal loyalties and personal choices.

Christian themes and tropes were deeply entrenched in many strands of the culture and continued to nourish sensibilities, especially compassion for the poor, a sense of the worth of the individual and of the importance of one's personal morality. But in business practice and political dealings, as well as most of the encounters of everyday living, these values were confined to moralising and sentimental self-deception. The Marxist dismissal of religion as 'the opium of the people' cut close to the bone. The only power the churches exercised in public life was to rally votes in favour of restricting indulgence in certain forms of sex, alcoholic drinks and gambling. Creative moral leadership in tackling social problems was not on their agenda.

The Catholic Church sought to adapt to the privatising of religion by building a set of institutions within which the faithful could live in relative isolation from the rest of the community. In the first half of the twentieth century in most English-speaking countries, and especially in Australia, this strategy was extraordinarily successful. An impressive network of churches, convents, schools, hospitals and charitable institutions was built, staffed and maintained entirely by the voluntary contributions of people who mostly belonged to the poorer sections of the population. The majority of Catholics went to mass every Sunday, funnelled any charitable activity through the church and socialised with other Catholics. Nearly every Catholic child went to a Catholic school that strove to provide an education at least as good as that of the state system without any assistance from the state. The supreme aim of the church was to keep the flock together under its own authority.

Critics of this enterprise spoke of the dangers of a ghetto mentality or a tribalism harking back to Irish nationalism. In practice these dangers were minimised by the conventionalist framework of Australia's secular culture. One had to conform to the framework of that culture, but the demands of conformity were neither exacting nor intrusive as far as most people were concerned. Their lives were lived on the scale of the nuclear family. For the most part, the sort of practical conformity that the church demanded was not to any program that impinged on other sections of the community but simply to building up its own institutions. In spiritual matters the church was avowedly authoritarian, but, except for its views on such matters as divorce and abortion, what it preached was seen as having little relevance to anything outside a person's private convictions. The prevailing culture had its critics, but they were usually also anti-Catholic. So Catholics tended to rally to the defence of the common culture, emphasising their loyalty to everything Australian.

One happy consequence of the particular structure of Australian conformism was that the ideological politics that was sweeping Europe had little purchase on Australian thinking and feeling. There was a lot wrong with the world, but it all came down to the actions of individuals. If everybody kept the rules, things would be all right. The rules were seen as the practical conventions that were the 'demands of society'. In the platitudes of the consensus the rules were given only the very vaguest, largely sentimental, religious significance. They were sanctified by a very minimalist version of the imperialist tradition, with its assumption that the 'more primitive races' would either come to adopt our Christian ways or be 'consigned to the dustbin of history'. Australia's role in history was celebrated and incarnated in our participation in the Great War, and by a mythology of mateship and rugged self-reliance.

Even in the depths of the Great Depression communism had little purchase on most Australians. They did not believe that life could be very much better than it already was in Australia. The key advantage of the Australian way of life was that one could lead one's own life and tell anybody who tried to interfere with that, or even to criticise one's choices, to go to hell. If there was any common good people strove to achieve or maintain, it was the unquestioning respect for that independence within the conventions. The way to safeguard it was not through political action but through everybody asserting their own independence in daily living and minding their own business. The standard matrix of life in this largely suburban society was the nuclear family in its own bungalow on its own fully fenced block of land. Pubs closed at 6pm to send men back to 'tea' at home. The sort of cafes or clubs in which people might socialise of an evening were non-existent. Most recreation consisted in watching sport, gambling and other individualistic activities. It was a flat, undifferentiated society, lacking the restless dynamism of its nearest relative, the USA. But it was very satisfied with itself.

Professional Training, Intellectual Tensions

The core of the first three years of a standard seminary training was philosophy, taught from a Latin textbook, authored and printed in Rome. Even the lectures were supposed to be given in Latin, though in practice a few sentences in Latin were followed by long explications in English. Those explanations failed completely to show why anybody should be interested in this stuff, except as the professional mumbo-jumbo that all professions seemed to need to exclude lay people from intruding into their domains. It was all utterly remote from live issues. In addition there was a course in the history of philosophy that was limited to schematic potted summaries that served to illustrate Descartes' saying that there was no idea so ridiculous that it had not been championed by some philosopher or other. Other courses introduced students to New Testament Greek, bits of English literature and ludicrously inadequate accounts of selected topics in psychology and social theory.

The philosophy itself was dreadful. At best it presented a poorly conceived simplification and amplification of certain themes of Aristotle. It was taught by men who said what they said because, according to ecclesiastical officialdom, that was the party line. Where the resemblance to official Marxism fell down was that the party line hardly ever changed. Indeed, the strongest claim to consideration that this philosophy could urge was that it was a sort of eternal truth, wholly immune to the influence of fashion. It presented a sort of commonsense view of the world as consisting of a lot of different substances, things like rocks and trees and animals, which each existed independently of the others and interacted as it did in virtue of its own nature or essence. That essence was the same in every member of a species, though differing in those superficial aspects called accidents.

This conception of the fundamental constituents of the real was completely at odds with modern physics, chemistry and biology. Fortunately that inconsistency could be ignored by taking a realist view of the categories of Aristotle and a conventionalist view of science. The categories of science were like the conventions in virtue of which some features of the curved surface of the earth could be represented on flat sheets of paper. Such conventions could be very useful for practical purposes, but they did not tell us anything about the real structure of things. This view was not entirely a pitiable evasion of some basic problems. Indeed, outside the seminary, it was fashionable among some idealist and phenomenalist philosophers, harking back to Bishop Berkeley. The atom bomb blew it apart.

Literary Influences

The advantage of the seminary regime in my eyes was that the standards it imposed were easy to meet and I could spend a lot of time reading outside the course material. In particular I was drawn to the writings of English Catholics, mainly converts, from Cardinal Newman through Hopkins and Patmore, Gilbert Chesterton and Hilaire Belloc down to Waugh and Greene. The prominence of so many converts was strong reassurance that the church did have the answers people were seeking. The rumbustious confidence of Chesterton and Belloc was particularly attractive to me. Their verse resonated with the familiar Australian bush ballads and the joyful enthusiasm of much of their writing gave me a new sense of the joy of believing.

It could not last. Chesterton in particular drew on an idealised pre-Reformation England for his distributism that prescribed a return to a society of robustly independent peasants as the remedy for the ills of the modern world. That was clearly both materially impossible and ideologically reactionary, oblivious of modern science and of all the positive achievements of modern culture. More fundamentally, the Chesterton–Belloc vision was theologically incoherent. They lampooned the earnest Victorian social reformers for their dreary propriety, they 'did not have the Faith and would not have the fun'. But fun meant women, wine and song in a frankly heathen spirit. The suggestion was that somehow the faith managed to reconcile uninhibited fun with the image of Christ on the cross. Belloc tried to spell it out in his *Heroic Poem in Praise of Wine*. In the end the devotee of Bacchus, addressing Jesus as 'comrade commander whom I daredst not earn', recalls how at the end he invited his disciples to share a cup of wine, he begs Jesus to share with him a chalice of that 'strong brother in God and last companion, wine', the pledge of a heaven to come.

Stirring stuff! But a travesty of the gospels, where what Jesus was doing at the last supper was leaving to the apostles his blood in the sacrament that was to re-enact forever the agonising sacrificial death he was about to undergo. The closer one looked at most English Catholicism, the more it became clear that the driving force behind it was a romantic rejection of the modern world that was neither a rebirth of Catholic tradition nor a profound insight into the contemporary situation. No wonder the exuberance of Chesterton and Belloc gave way to the ambivalences and uncertainties of Greene and Waugh, whose insights into the contemporary world were so much more incisive and revealing, but hardly very encouraging.

Moral Theology and Its Discontents

Advancing from philosophy to the four years of theology was seen as a great step forward into areas that were of genuine pastoral concern.

The core subjects were dogmatic theology, explicating and defending the doctrines of the church; moral theology, directed mainly to giving guidance, especially in the confessional, about where to draw the line on what was permitted and the line between venial and mortal sin; scripture, concentrating on philological New Testament exegesis; and canon law, dealing with ecclesiastical legislation, which had been codified, European style, earlier in the century. Ecclesiastical history and pastoral theology were tacked on. The teaching at this level was much more professional and competent by the lights of the tradition in which it situated itself. But that tradition was deeply unsatisfactory in many respects and destined to be called into question less than twenty years later in the Second Vatican Council.

The most obviously deficient subject was moral theology, conceived legalistically as casuistry. The irreverent described it as 'the art of sinning without breaking God's law'. The standard position on what was permitted was probabilism. Against the rigorists who argued that one could not act on any principle that was less than certain, for fear of doing the wrong thing, the probabilists argued that you were entitled to do anything that an approved author regarded as permissible. The presumption was in favour of liberty, and in this respect legalistic probabilism was salutary. (Interestingly, this was the origin of the notion of probability. Acting on an opinion that was less than certain was permissible if the opinion was 'probabilis', Latin for 'approvable'. The term came to be extended to cover the notion of reasonable risk and then to the calculation of chances.) In almost any area other than sexual morality one could find opinions that allowed a great deal of leeway, especially in matters of obligations in justice or arising out of civil law or custom. One was not expected to take the initiative in righting wrongs, even those one caused, especially if it involved disgracing or impoverishing oneself. Obligations in charity were largely matters of 'supererogation', worthy, but entirely optional. On the other hand, even a deliberately entertained 'impure thought' was a mortal sin, let alone any sexual act other than the sort of intercourse within marriage that was open to procreation. The salient peculiarity about rules on sex was probably not just the celibacy of the legislators but also the fact that in sexual conduct it was easy to draw hard and fast lines about physical activities, while in non-physical matters it was not possible to do so. The cultivation of virtue, concern about the sort of person one aspired to be, or concern to act for the good of others, even of all humankind, had no place in this discourse. These were matters of personal choice, of supererogation.

The legalistic conception of divine law resembled the conventionalist view of morality. In the one case one spoke of the demands of society, in the other of the demands of God. In both cases the focus was less on the point and spirit of the law than on the more or less arbitrary imposition it placed on the individual in the interests of some wider social or transcendent order that the ordinary subject of the law was not expected to understand. Exceptions could not be made, even where there seemed to be good reason for them, because the rule must be upheld. People must not be allowed to judge in matters they did not understand, and the rules must be as clear and as uncontested as possible. Such moralities did not envisage serious social choices.

One of the positive outcomes of the atrocities of the Second World War was to generate a new conception of moral seriousness. The criminals of the death camps could not be excused on the ground that they were acting in accordance with the conventions of their society. Even to condemn them as disobeying the law of God seemed too remote and superficial. Surely God condemned them, as some of them came to blame themselves, because of the morally repugnant character of what they did. A viable morality had to come to grips not just with rules about right and wrong but with good and evil. One traditional Catholic account of the basis of morality was the doctrine of natural law, of which there were many variants. The basic idea was that every creature has a purpose inscribed in its nature by the creator. Beings that lack intelligence fulfil that purpose blindly, through natural necessity, but human beings, having free will, need to understand and conform voluntarily to the true purpose of their various abilities. Speech is for communicating truth. So lying is wrong. Sex is for procreation and frustrating procreation is wrong. And so on.

Take a narrow view of the purpose of each activity and you arrive at a very repressive pattern. Almost anything we can do can have incidental uses that seem very legitimate. Eating and drinking for pleasure rather than nourishment seems perfectly harmless in moderation, provided our overall diet is healthy and nourishing. So why must each and every sexual activity be open to procreation, especially as it is not claimed that everybody has an obligation to marry and procreate? In practice Catholic theologians took a rigorist line on the teleology of sex and a liberal line on almost everything else, for no very convincing reason.

More fundamentally, the natural law tradition in attempting to ground moral prescriptions in its metaphysics of nature, neglected the deep and specific ways in which the significance of every element of people's lives depended on the culture in which their identities were grounded. On the one hand it failed to appreciate the crucial importance of the constructive differences of meaning that various natural functions and pervasive institutions developed in different circumstances. On the other it tended to impoverish critical analysis of the deficiencies of various cultures by attacking them on the basis of a simplistic teleology instead of looking to the rich possibilities of development that social groups might discover in learning from each other.

The case of usury supplies a simple example of these dangers. Medieval opinion almost unanimously condemned charging for lending money, though it allowed that charging rent on real estate was legitimate. The argument was that money was inherently 'unproductive'. It was assumed that its purpose was consumption, and that people only borrowed because of their need, usually dire need, for the necessities of life. So charging interest on money lent was to exploit the borrower. Eventually, as mercantilism and capitalism became the dominant modes of production, various ways of justifying interest on money for productive investment were found, until finally money was seen as a commodity like any other and the fallacy of dogmatising about 'money as such' was abandoned. Unfortunately the obsession of the clergy with a dogmatic view of the nature of sexual relations was not open to discussion.

It took me a long time to work my way out of the natural law tradition, as we shall see in due course. It was, of course, not just an academic matter, but involved questioning the authority of the official church over the consciences of its members and the relation of Christians to the modern world. Was Christianity to be 'the Light of the World', a source of moral progress, or a hanging judge, determined to condemn it in order to enforce an indefensibly rigid law? It was becoming increasingly obvious that the fight against social evils in modern times, against racism, exploitation, slavery and tyranny, had been led not by the church, but by secular humanists. The best one could claim was that in doing so they were drawing on the resources of Christian tradition.

Dogmatism about Dogma

Dogmatic theology was not much better. It consisted mainly in interpreting scripture and tradition in terms of the categories and principles of Roman Thomism, the arid and myopic version of the thought of Aquinas developed in the Pontifical Universities in Rome. Theologically it impoverished the rich tradition on which it drew. Philosophically it was often ridiculous. The besetting sin of this version of Thomism was to reify everything it touched, especially treating nonmaterial entities as if they were components of material things. Recourse to analogies drawn from sensory experience in attempting to elucidate metaphysical and spiritual matters is inevitable, but it must be qualified always by an acute awareness of the danger of being misled, dogmatising metaphors as if they were literal truth. Everybody conceded that we could talk of spiritual realities only through analogies, but in practice certain privileged analogies were pushed to extremes.

The received view of analogy was that it consisted in a 'proportionality': A is to B as C is to D. To take a numerical example, if A is to 6 as 2 is to 4, then A=3. Such analogies have uses everywhere. The mathematics of wave functions enable physicists to describe certain subatomic phenomena, and so on. But when one says that God's relation to us is like that of father to child, it is crucial to remember that God is infinitely different from us. There is no common measure between creator and creature, according to Christian theology. So there is no question of making due allowance for the differences between them, much less of calculating exactly what they entail. The Roman Thomists knew and acknowledged that, of course, but in practice they regularly disregarded it.

They were obsessed with the need to insist that Catholic dogmas were literally true, not just metaphorical pointers to mysteries beyond human comprehension. The thrust was avowedly authoritarian. Truth demanded assent. The authority to decide what is true and what is false is the ultimate form of authority, vested in the infallibility of the pope. The Roman theologians saw their task as that of construing the truths of Catholic doctrine in formulae that were as unequivocal and as clear as possible. So they were driven inexorably to take what were at best metaphors[2] as if they were

2 I use the term metaphor in its vaguest sense to cover all cognitive content that is not to be assessed as a matter of literal truth. Obviously the boundary between the two is highly contentious, but the broad contrast seems inescapable and primordial. In characterising statements as metaphor I do not want to suggest that they are arbitrary or vacuous. I attach great importance to the work of Gaston Bachelard, the great French philosopher of science, who also wrote a series of fascinating books exploring the domain of what he called poetics, with titles like *The Psychoanalysis of Fire* and *The Poetics of Space*, in which he emphasised that

statements of fact, to draw out every strand of an analogy, heedless of its limitations, and to treat as established truth the most dubious conceptions of scholasticism.

A simple example of the temptation to reification was the doctrine of sanctifying grace. Luther had protested that we always remain sinners, saved only by the son of God offering himself up on our behalf to bear the punishment we deserve. Grace does not change us, but draws a veil over our wickedness. Counter-Reformation doctrine, by contrast, insisted that grace was a real causal power that transforms us inwardly from sinners into saints, even if that transformation is never complete in this life. And what was called 'actual grace', the sort of divine assistance one might seek in a moment of temptation, was described as a 'praemotio physica', a physical push, though of a spiritual, not material, nature, that launched one in the right direction! It would be tedious and pointless to elaborate on the absurdities that these authors found themselves committed to in their attempt to pin down the mysteries of religion by turning metaphors into literal truths.

I came to argue that, in spite of occasional incautious slips, Aquinas was largely free from such damning faults. For a while I thought that what was needed was a closer fidelity to the subtleties of Aquinas' thinking that were obscured by the crude literalism of the Roman theologians. But the more I read Aquinas and his disciples, the more I came to think that what needed to be done was not to systematise his thinking in a more rigorous way but to open

---

the poetic image has not only an intersubjective reality but what he called a trans-subjective force. It is not just a matter of our projecting purely subjective feelings onto physical things. Objective truth imposes itself on us, just like the forces it represents independently of our feelings about it. Metaphor at its best draws us towards an understanding, but only to the extent that we respond sympathetically to its content. The practical difference is that objective truth can have an authority that does not attach to metaphor, however important its content. It is characteristic of authoritarianism to attempt to extend illegitimately the domain of objective truth.

up a dialogue with modern thought, as he had opened up theology to dialogue with Aristotle and the Arab thinkers. Later I would discover that the tendencies to dogmatise, to reduce complex, many-faceted matters to a few allegedly fundamental categories and make exaggerated claims in the name of truth were by no means confined to Roman theologians. Reification and reductionism of one sort or another was endemic in the Western philosophical tradition. Each philosophical position wanted to set up an exclusive set of categories and to claim that their particular set of boxes accommodated everything that was really real, in spite of the fact that they never got any closer to agreeing about who had the right set of boxes, much less what needed to fit into them and what could be dismissed as unreal.

None of this dissatisfaction with official policy in theoretical and practical matters had much effect on my spiritual life. I performed my duties, said my prayers and scrutinised my own motivations in accordance with approved practice. Every Christian was supposed to follow the example of the master, but in a particular way priests as ministers of the gospel and the altar were required to conform as closely as possible to what Jesus would have done in their situation. So one of the key practices enjoined on candidates for the priesthood was a period of prayerful meditation on some scene from the gospels, attempting to come closer to the master by enriching one's imagination with a vivid sense of his personality, his virtues and his concerns. Those sources were inexhaustible and any individual could hope to reflect a very partial aspect of them. There was room for a great many different interpretations from different points of view and for a good deal of creativity in relating to new challenges.

The Life of a Priest

At the breakfast for relatives and friends following my ordination in October 1949, I announced that I saw my particular mission as lying in 'the thinking business', a way of referring to philosophy that strove not to sound too pretentious. I hoped to go overseas to study. Meanwhile I was posted as curate to the parish of Maroubra Bay, under the parish priest, Dominic Furlong. Dom was a genial, though somewhat twitchy character, who came from a family of prosperous publicans. His most prominent characteristic was a spontaneous sympathy with the concerns of his parishioners and the warmth and insight of the ways in which he conveyed it to them. What mattered to him above all was the quality of one's personal relations with people. Working with him was a salutary corrective for somebody preoccupied with abstract matters.

In addition to the routine pastoral work of visiting the sick or troubled and attempting to round up those who had strayed from the fold, I became involved with some laymen and a couple of other priests in the work of The Catholic Evidence Guild, standing up 'on the soapbox' in public places such as the Sydney Domain to explain to casual passers-by what the Catholic position on this or that was. Since anybody who mounted the soapbox was regarded as a ratbag by common consent, many saw this activity as demeaning to the cloth. But then there was ample evidence in the gospels that many respectable people took Jesus as a ratbag for much the same reasons. The goal was not so much to contact and convert individuals to Catholicism, but to show that we had something we were anxious to offer to everybody.

One of the moving spirits behind the guild, at first in Sydney, but by this time in London, was Frank Sheed, who belonged to a new breed of lay Catholic intellectuals, distinctly different from the traditional literary figures like Chesterton and Belloc. Sheed was in fact a lay theologian. In London Sheed married Maisie Ward, from a prominent English family that became Catholic in the wake of the nineteenth-century Oxford Movement in the Church of England. They founded the publishing house Sheed and Ward which in the thirties and forties brought new vigour to Catholic publishing in English, by translating some of the most innovative French and

German writers and encouraging young writers in English. The emphasis was on theological, philosophical and social themes, treated in an idiom that was free of the jargon and pretentions of official theology and spoke to contemporary concerns. I was an enthusiastic admirer of their work.

This interest in confronting the world with the message of the faith set me apart somewhat from my clerical colleagues, who saw themselves as pastors of the flock committed to their care. The wide world was not their responsibility. They had enough on their plate. Sensible though it was, this attitude could take dangerously simplistic forms, as it did, I believed, in the case of Norman Thomas Cardinal Gilroy, the first Australian Archbishop of Sydney. Gilroy's sole criterion in judging any organisation or policy was how it affected the interests of the church, especially its short-term financial interests or its social standing. He used to say 'God loves the church more than we do', interpreting that to mean that all he need worry about was the administrative responsibility of running a tightly controlled organisation. He would hear no evil concerning corrupt politicians or dubious entrepreneurs if they did the church the odd favour, while refusing to believe anything to the credit of those he saw as its adversaries. This attitude could, and in several cases did, lead to notoriously corrupt police and politicians enjoying the aura of 'devout Catholics', and to a fixed determination to hush up any abuse which revealed might 'create a scandal'.

Running a tight organisation meant keeping the laity in their place. Under the name 'Catholic Action', somewhat ambivalently and tepidly endorsed by the hierarchy, a number of lay organisations, modelled on European, particularly French, initiatives, had sprung up, promoting what they saw as Catholic answers to the problems of the day. Young Christian Workers, Catholic Rural Movement, Social Justice and so on were particularly strong in Melbourne, under the protection of Archbishop Mannix, the canny old Irish patrician, who was never averse to stirring things up a little. Most such organisations were kept out of Sydney. True, some of the ideas they were used to promote were very debatable, but the idea that the solution to the problems that were posed by people claiming theological warrant for questionable ideas lay in vigorous and uncensored debate was anathema to Gilroy and those around him. Suppression was their answer.

Paradoxically, this unattractive authoritarianism worked to Gilroy's advantage when, in the early fifties, under the leadership of Bob Santamaria, head of the romantic Catholic Rural Movement, a semi-clandestine organisation was formed in Victoria to fight the communists who were seen as about to get control of the unions and the Labor Party. It had disastrous results, culminating in the split in 1954 that disabled the Labor Party for many years to come. Gilroy did his utmost to stop the movement spreading to NSW and gained credit in many eyes for keeping the church out of politics, or at least not giving ammunition to sectarianism.

3

GRAPPLING WITH PHILOSOPHY: CRUMBLING FOUNDATIONS

The opportunity to go overseas for further study arrived in the middle of 1951. A senior Irish priest endowed a scholarship to send a Sydney priest to study at St Patrick's College, Maynooth, the major seminary of Ireland and a college of the National University of Ireland, along with the University Colleges of Dublin, Cork and Galway. I was in sufficiently good standing to be granted this opportunity. It was only many years later that priests such as Paul Crittenden and Julian Miller were allowed to go to Oxford.

I sailed to the UK on the old P&O liner *Strathmore*. For five weeks I was for the first time as an adult in entirely lay, mostly non-Catholic company. I dressed in clerical garb except in the hottest weather, celebrated mass each morning in the tourist lounge and soon found that I attracted like flies people who wanted to give me their views on religion or to narrate their life history. On a relatively small ship it was not easy to avoid the bores, particularly if one was self-conscious about the dangers of giving offence. But there were compensations. I made the acquaintance of Ian Hogbin, an anthropologist from Sydney University, whose interest in baroque art amounted almost to an obsession. Later in Sydney we were to become firm friends, but for the moment the young cleric felt uncouth and ignorant in the company of the very sophisticated and knowledgeable academic. Ian was a forceful and courageous character. The risks he took and hardships he endured in his fieldwork in New Guinea were amazing, especially given his fastidious tastes. He made no attempt to hide his homosexuality at a time when homosexual intercourse was still a crime that some police prosecuted with zeal. It almost certainly cost him the chair of anthropology at Sydney.

The highlights of the voyage were stops at Colombo, Bombay, Aden (as they were then), Suez and Marseilles, each of which, excepting Marseilles, provided a challenging glimpse of people and places that were still immersed in the colonial era. Colombo seemed relaxed in tropical luxuriance and an easy-going Buddhism, but Bombay was deeply shocking, with its mutilated child-beggars, streets of downtrodden prostitutes and atmosphere of turmoil. Aden and Suez were unglamorous oriental bazaars, where indefatigable touts sold fake watches to tourists who couldn't resist a bargain. There was an enormous gap to be bridged, I thought, before these places would become part of the world system. It was only much later that I came to realise that they were already fully integrated into that order, but in roles that were not of their own choosing, and that the comfortable assumptions of Anglo-Australian colonialism needed to be radically reassessed.

Ireland in 1951 was a very dreary place, as was its British neighbour. The shadows of the Civil War thirty years earlier still cast a divisive gloom over politics and society. The cant of hero-worship and betrayal was endlessly regurgitated by political hacks, to the disgust of the younger generation. The economy was still almost wholly based on very small and inefficient farms. Eldest sons waited into middle age for their fathers to die and leave them the farm, thus permitting them to marry in middle age. Other children, having little prospect of employment or marriage and a very restricted social life, emigrated to the England of postwar austerity, which was in some respects less tolerable than that of wartime, a matter of national poverty rather than willing sacrifice. The church, which conceived its message and organisation in the narrowest terms, had a stranglehold on education and the politics of sexual behaviour. No condoms on sale, no divorce and so on. Censorship of print, stage and screen was ludicrously strict.

Nevertheless, private life among the well-off, including the clergy, could be very agreeable, and I found a number of friends among them. I acquired a somewhat battered second-hand Austin A40, saw a good deal of the country and enjoyed its hospitality. I became particularly fond of the dry, sceptical wit of some of my colleagues. When around the fire on a winter evening an earnest young priest went on about the virtues of the current pope, Pius XII, a colleague cut him short with the remark: 'Sure, and ain't he well paid for it!' Another entertained us with a literary appraisal of the couplet:

> Knee deep in the gorse
> Stood the homosexual horse.

The seeds of the great resurgence of Ireland in the following generation were beginning to sprout.

In the summer of 1952 I took the old Austin on a European grand tour, with the assistance of various passengers, clerical and lay, who helped with expenses and contacts who would provide hospitality. Young Australians were travelling to Europe in unprecedented numbers and being welcomed by people who were just as interested to learn about the antipodes as those from 'down under' were to find out about Europe. Respectable young ladies from Adelaide hitchhiked all over Europe, finding a warm welcome everywhere. There was a sense throughout Europe that the old Europe had been a political and social disaster and that only a radical change of attitudes and structures could ensure that the horrors of the recent past could never be repeated. The movement towards European Union, comprehensive social security and respect for the humanity of people in all their variety had begun. The experience of this renewal had a profound influence on my faith, confirming my sense that the church as a community was entering a new and positive age. Clearly, the social movement in Europe was driven by a renewal of Christian consciousness in which the virtues of faith, hope and charity were being given a social and political significance that transcended the narrow, sentimental and formalistic practices of a church focused exclusively on the 'salvation of souls'. It was no longer a question of rescuing and isolating 'souls' from the world, the flesh and the devil, but of building a set of social relations that would reflect and sustain a life in accordance with the message of the gospels.

Maynooth and Bertrand Russell

At Maynooth I was granted a BA *ad eundum gradum* in recognition of my seminary studies and enrolled in an MA course. Maynooth was not noted for its philosophy courses, and I was the only postgraduate student of the subject, but there were several competent lecturers in the subject who helped sympathetically my frantic efforts to acquire a comprehensive background in contemporary British philosophy. My attention soon focused on the stream that issued from the work of Bertrand Russell. I commenced a thesis on Russell's theories of scientific inference. What interested me particularly was Russell's attempt to ground all sound inference in mathematics, which in turn rested on the new propositional logic that he had done more than anyone else to develop. The new logic was claimed to supplant and subsume the traditional syllogistic logic that had come down almost without change or major development from the work of Aristotle.

I came to the view that the internal difficulties in Russell's philosophy invalidated not only the specific theses he advanced but the project that he and most of his contemporaries identified as the prime task of philosophy, in accordance with tradition going back to the seventeenth century, particularly to Descartes. The problem was that modern science had begun to reveal with increasing clarity and certainty that sensory perception and the concepts based on it were not a sound guide to the nature of the physical world. What we perceive as colours are not properties of the surfaces of things or even of rays of light, but reactions caused in us by causes of a very different kind. And so on for the other sensory properties of things. We live in a world, including our own bodies, which operates at the level of its fundamental constituents in ways that we could not suspect if guided by mere commonsense. The task, then, is to show how we are to understand our place in this world. Just what kind of beings are we really? Are we just physical systems or something quite different? What sort of knowledge can we have? How is it to be validated?

It seemed obvious that to answer such questions satisfactorily it was not enough to appeal to what seemed obvious to us, much less to construct explanations in terms of spiritual agencies, as ancient and medieval philosophers so often did. It was necessary to find a firm, unquestionable foundation for our knowledge, preferably one that is objectively self-validating, necessarily true. Having found the foundation we could build up a rational reconstruction of our knowledge. Clearly the history of human knowledge, even of science was very messy, full of lucky guesses, half-understood truths and the like. What philosophers needed to show is how to judge impartially what our claims to knowledge are really worth. The subtext usually was that men (women didn't matter so much) should be freed from false beliefs, which were responsible for most of the problems of mankind.

Descartes believed that the indubitable basis of all our knowledge was our inability to doubt our own existence as spiritual beings. He assumed that mind was transparent to itself in a way that matter could not be. That assumption itself was soon thrown into doubt. British empiricists tended to think that the only irrefragable data were sense-data, particular sensory impressions like colour patches, sounds, smells and shapes. Russell largely went along with this contention, but he was much more impressed by our knowledge of logic and mathematics, which, in common with many other twentieth-century Anglophone philosophers, he believed to be necessarily true, true in all possible worlds and self-validating. In one of the great works of their time, called *Principia Mathematica* (3 vols, 1910, 1912, 1913) in imitation of Newton, their great Cambridge predecessor, he and AN Whitehead set out to show how the whole of mathematics could be derived from logic, which in turn was self-validating. The project ran into problems that could be avoided only by placing seemingly arbitrary restrictions on what counted as a correctly formulated proposition in the system. Eventually Kurt Gödel, an Austrian mathematician, demonstrated that no system powerful enough to do what Russell wanted to do could guarantee its own consistency. The search for a self-validating ground for knowledge was doomed to fail.

The position, then, was that neither pure a priori mathematics nor sense data could jointly or singly provide the sort of basis that the rational reconstruction project required. Russell was reluctant to give up the project altogether. So he turned with some misgivings to evolutionary and pragmatic explanations of the process of acquisition of knowledge in his last major work, *Human Knowledge*. The only live competitors seemed unacceptable. Among the most popular was the view of Karl Popper that science was a matter of conjectures and refutations. What we regard as knowledge is simply a set of conjectures that have not so far been refuted. The more traditional alternative was to postulate some form of innate knowledge that would bridge the gap between inadequate evidence and the conclusions it was deemed to support. Both positions were unsatisfactory. Popper could not explain how positive evidence supported some conclusions much more than others, while the purveyors of a priori principles of induction simply postulated arbitrarily whatever they thought was needed. Unfortunately, Russell's use of evolution was subject to much the same objections.

I concluded that the whole problematic, the interlocking set of problems around the 'foundationalist' enterprise, was mistaken. It rested on an individualist conception of all knowledge as a matter of solitary intuition, an immediate unity or even identity between the knowing subject and the object known. It depended on trying to understand knowledge on the analogy of isolated episodes of vision. Such episodes can be rich as experiences, but they are not the content of objective knowledge. Their importance lies elsewhere. We treasure them in memory and attempt to express their particular force and resonances in the arts. Communicating them to others depends on the power of our forms of expression to evoke in them the sense of that experience. When we are not concentrating on the aesthetic content of sensory experience it functions mainly as signals alerting us to events to which we need to pay selective attention, depending on what we are doing. What matters is not the content of the experience but its practical function in our interactions with the world. We are constantly reacting to sensory information both consciously and unconsciously, using inbuilt or acquired skills to handle it. But this sort of knowledge is a matter of personal attainments, most notably in the skills of the craftsman. It is limited in comparison to knowledge in what I shall call 'the strong sense'. It can be acquired only by practice and its secrets are easily lost.

We know something in the strong sense of the word when we understand a true proposition and believe it to be true for good reasons. Propositional knowledge can be recorded and integrated into formulae that link it with a network of interconnections not only with the thoughts and actions of other people, but with the physical world. Propositional knowledge can often be embodied in physical apparatus to generate further knowledge and applied by standard procedures to situations beyond human experience, as when cosmologists generate precise, testable explanations of the origins of the universe. The individualist model neglects the indispensable role of language as the intersubjective bearer of the concepts through which experience is understood and of the techniques and skills by which it is sought, manipulated and used, for complex calculations as well as in interpersonal contexts. Language is very much more than just a means of people signalling to each other.

Contemporary English-speaking philosophy was rightly impressed by the extraordinary achievements and possibilities of objective knowledge, but it tended to treat it as self-contained, logically independent of those ordinary forms of interaction with our environment on which it depends in practice. To abstract from the social and psychological contexts and the varieties of kinds of knowledge was to pose pseudo-problems, as if one were to attempt to explain how a baby might be born without a mother. It may well be the case that we will learn how to produce babies without mothers, but only by understanding how mothers do it. I was increasingly drawn to the contemporary Oxford 'ordinary language' philosophers who saw the task of philosophy as conceptual analysis, especially articulating clearly neglected distinctions and relationships among the concepts, institutionalised in ordinary linguistic practice, that lie behind our ordinary dealings with the world and each other. Philosophy, thus understood posed no great threat to faith. It did not demand impossible justifications for belief or present an allegedly objective metaphysical view of the world from which God was excluded.

Louvain and Frege

Having completed the MA in 1953, I raised the question of progression to a PhD. The Maynooth authorities did not feel they had the resources to support a PhD student and agreed to write to my Sydney sponsor suggesting that I be allowed to go to the Catholic University of Louvain in Belgium, the usual progression for Irish priests. The proposal was accepted with the proviso that I could only take a year more leave from the diocese. So I was faced with the problem of coping with seventeen semester courses and writing a PhD thesis in one year. Somehow I managed, under the supervision of the very congenial Canon Robert Feys, a distinguished logician as well as an authority on English Romantic poetry.

As my thesis topic I chose Gottlob Frege's theory of logic, partly because the literature on the topic was small enough to be manageable, but also because in the eyes of key players in Oxford and Cambridge Frege's analysis of language and logic was very much superior to Russell's and indeed anybody else's. Frege was a relatively obscure German mathematician with little philosophical background, but a strong interest in the foundations of mathematics. He came to attention in England because, working on the same problems as Russell, he corresponded with him.

Meanwhile I took a brief holiday and an opportunity to brush up my schoolboy French at a summer school on Christianity and politics organised by the Catholic Institute of Toulouse at a very pleasant site overlooking Ustaritz in the Pyrenees. The organisers had managed to enlist a number of prominent French intellectuals and attract a full complement of students from France, Germany, Belgium and even Scotland. It further confirmed and illustrated my perception of what was happening in the church in Europe, as well as reinforcing my love of France.

I went to Louvain six weeks before term began to get a flying start on the task ahead, taking lodgings over a drugstore opposite the Institute of Philosophy and just around the corner from the famous library. The lodgings had no provision for meals or bathing and I was reduced to eating out and imposing on the American College for a bath once a week. Among those I met in Louvain was Ernan McMullin, a priest from Donegal, who was later to become an influential figure in American philosophy as an expert in the philosophy of science and the head of department chiefly responsible for turning the philosophy department of the University of Notre Dame into a highly professional institution. Later we were to translate together a work of one of the bright lights of Louvain, Albert Dondeyne's *Contemporary European Thought and Christian Faith*, which presented a form of Christian existentialism. Soon after I arrived I received a letter from Max Charlesworth from Melbourne who was about to arrive in Louvain with his wife and baby to undertake a PhD asking me to look for accommodation for them. What I found was a flat over a 'blue' cinema run by two very nice old ladies. Max and I became firm friends.

The courses I was required to take consisted almost wholly of lectures and required little reading and no writing. Louvain was a medieval foundation that had survived to become the largest and internationally best-known university in Belgium. It still carried a good deal of medieval heritage, notably a strong clerical element in the faculty, especially in key positions, though with a long tradition of independence from the Vatican. Another medieval relic was the curious requirement that all examinations should be public examinations, ideally at an announced time before an audience of anybody who was interested. In practice they were still oral, but usually in private in the lecturer's study. This, too, mitigated the course requirements, since it was often possible to turn a question into a discussion and display what one knew about the subject rather than reveal one's ignorance. The system imposed a terrible burden on Feys. Because the enrolments in logic were small he was required to lecture on philosophy to 1600 conscript engineering and science students and then to give each of them a quarter-hour oral examination.

The leading interests in Louvain were in phenomenology and existentialism. The university had custody of the archives of Husserl, the founder of phenomenology, and strong contacts with both French and German developments, though I had little opportunity to follow up such leads. The main influence on me, other than Feys, was the great Aristotelian scholar, Auguste Mansion, who taught me to read Aristotle without interpolating the distorting commentary of Aquinas.

The work on Frege was very technical and the jury of examiners gave me a doctorate with 'grande distinction' mainly because they were impressed by Feys's assurance that I had succeeded in mastering a notoriously difficult German's idiosyncratic concepts and notation. One of the principal legacies of Frege to subsequent discussion was his distinction between the sense and the reference of expressions. 'Walter Scott' and 'the author of Waverley' both refer to the same person, but their sense is different. Hitherto the distinction had been neglected because of the tendency to treat all logical relations in terms of the extension of class membership. So to say this ball is black is simply to say that it is a member of both the class of balls and the class of black things. Frege showed that this way of dealing with the matter might work in certain limited contexts, but was radically inadequate for most purposes, and his work in doing so opened up new vistas in understanding logic and language. The role of concepts was very much more complex and constructive than merely tagging objects with labels.

It so happened that two of the best interpreters of Frege were two prominent Catholics, Peter Geach, professor at Leeds, married to Elizabeth Anscombe of Oxford, of whom more anon, and Michael Dummett, also of Oxford. Geach and Dummett both responded generously to my requests for enlightenment on several points and encouraged me to think that I was on the right track to contribute to renewing relations between philosophy and Christian belief. They were particularly insistent on the objective importance of conceptual questions, of making clear and appropriate distinctions and not being misled by simplistic analogies. I found their robust objectivity much more congenial that the vague existentialism of Dondeyne's work. Dummett was later to go on to be a professor at Oxford and a philosopher of great influence, in spite of having taken two years off academic work to devote himself to fighting Britain's racist immigration rules and assisting their victims. The central point that I took from these and other contemporary British philosophers was the complexity of the ways in which linguistic forms related to the situations to which they applied. That complexity was misconstrued when it was forced into arbitrarily privileged categories that gave rise to pseudo-problems.

A New Direction in Philosophy

In her important but short book *Intention* (1957), Anscombe showed how the description of an action as intentional or even deliberate did not authorise its analysis into two separable components, a physical action and an inner mental event of acquiring an intention that caused the action. Nor did it authorise the elimination of the mental as some unobservable subjective accompaniment of observable behaviour. The significance of intentional actions could be understood only through their relations to the contexts of their use in different aspects of human life. Both introspection and observation of particular events taken in isolation occluded the interpersonal relationships and practices that gave intentional actions their special character. As I understood this contention, it was not intended to exclude the undeniable existence of private episodes in which we might decide to do something at a later date, or perhaps change our minds, without any overt behaviour. What it meant was that these activities were only possible in virtue of our already having the concept of overt intentional action. They were not pure or basic cases of forming an intention but rather interior rehearsals of overt action that had to be understood in the light of the action they foreshadowed. To postulate a separate mental event of forming an intention as the necessary prior cause of each intentional action produced an entirely misleading conception of the relations between mind and matter.

More generally the tide was running strongly against reductionism, the enterprise of trying to show that what appeared to be different kinds of things were really the same, once one got beyond superficial appearances. The point of reductionism was the ambition to find what is 'really real', show how our view of the cosmos and of ourselves could get behind mere appearances and reach genuine wisdom. In its most general form reductionism was as old as philosophy itself. The urge to dismiss inconvenient aspects of experience, such as suffering or sickness, as illusory is ubiquitous. Many philosophies have treated the material world as an illusionary veil over the truly real world of spirit. On the other hand materialists have insisted that only material things have effects in reality. In modern times reductionism has been reinforced and given a more precise form in emulation of the physical sciences, especially physics itself. Physics has been spectacularly successful in showing how the properties of complexes can be explained in terms of the apparently quite different properties of their constituents. Individual molecules cannot be hot, but the heat of a complex piece of matter can be explained completely in terms of the interactions of the molecules of which it is composed. Life can be explained on the basis of the properties of the nonliving constituents of living things, and so on.

Of course, what physics shows is not that life is an illusion or that heat does not exist. On the contrary, living things are very different from inanimate things in numerous respects and understanding life has become possible only by fuller analysis of its specific components, such as reproduction, growth and death. Until the specific peculiarities of heat were understood in terms of the laws of thermodynamics, the kinetic theory of heat was mere conjecture. Genuine, detailed reductive explanations are important in many ways. In particular, they show that it is a mistake to think of heat as a distinct force in addition to such forces as gravitational attraction or electromagnetism, which, provisionally, may be taken as irreducible in terms of a certain stage of physical theory. Similarly we now accept that the age-old assumption that living things are enlivened by some sort of immaterial soul, conceived as a causal operator of a very different kind from the forces that constitute inanimate matter, is quite unfounded. The results of physics teach us astounding, utterly unexpected things about how the world works, how it came to develop into the world we know and how we fit into its evolution.

In doing so it makes a lot of profound differences in the way we interact with the world and the terms in which we think about it.

Explanations of particular events as the result of secret decisions and powers of postulated intentional agents are no longer plausible. Magic, witchcraft, fairies, goblins and ghosts are consigned to imaginary worlds. God survives in spite of the demise of other spiritual beings in view of the deep mystery of his purposes and his transcendental power. Invoked to provide the ultimate explanation of everything, he is relieved of explaining anything in particular. As a philosophical theory theism is full of difficulties and paradoxes, but that is true of every known type of ultimate explanation. Still the idea of everything other than the creator being explained in terms of an ultimate, unconditioned choice whose content is wholly explained in terms of the ends to which it is directed seems coherent enough. What no longer seems defensible is the idea that there *must* be such an ultimate explanation. It is perfectly conceivable that as each universe dies it implodes into the next big bang.

The metaphysical principle of causality on which traditional proofs of god's existence rely is also false. It is not true that an entity's acquiring a certain property must be explained by its being conferred on that entity by some superior entity that has that property. Even at the level of ordinary experience we know that water turns into ice as a result of temperature changes, not because of some hard agent conferring hardness on it. Now evolutionary theory enables us to understand that design does not need to involve a designer. Of course it might involve a designer, even if that hypothesis can no longer be claimed to be necessary.

What could convert this abstract possibility into an urgent question? It is no longer plausible to claim to read the natural history of creation as manifesting God's intentions. These could be known only to the extent that he revealed them explicitly. There is no way of discerning to what precise ends the universe is directed, especially if those ends lie beyond the perishable world in which we live. Our best accounts suggest that evolution is blind. I came to accept that not just the specific claims of this or that religion, but the very existence of theistic religion as a basic dimension of the universe now depends on the strength of some claim to there being a divine revelation. How might we go about assessing such a claim?

It seems possible to conceive of an originating choice that is explained wholly in terms of the end to which it is directed. So I argued we must admit that if there were such a creator, it would not only be conceivable, but likely that he would choose to reveal his purposes. Suppose, for example, that on every TV or computer screen in the world the same serious message appeared in the language of the viewer, claiming to be the word of God, it would be hard to resist that claim. As one of my atheist friends admitted, 'give me a miracle like that and I'll be on my knees in a flash'. In other words, it seems conceivable that there could be such a thing as a convincing claim to divine revelation. What, then of existing claims? Traditional reliance on the miracles of Jesus seems weak in the light of historical criticism and of our awareness that there are many apparently inexplicable events that are not claimed as evidence for extraordinary powers. Evaluations of claims to reveal God's purposes need to relate more closely to the actual content of those claims and in particular to whether they were credible.

It seemed clear to me that the outstanding candidate among competing claims to embody such a revelation was the Catholic Church, and that in the long run that claim can be tested only in terms of its capacity in practice to live up to its own claims, to manifest its redeeming message in action. Those claims, as St Paul acknowledged from the beginning, are hardly sustainable as common sense. But it is hardly plausible, given what we know of the disconcerting character of our universe, that a set of vaguely common sense platitudes could be a plausible candidate for the role of a divine revelation. Such a revelation had to be specific and utterly surprising by conventional standards. So it had to claim authority, a recognisable, embodied organ through which it was continually proclaimed and interpreted as objectively true. In the long run only the Catholic Church made that claim universally, persistently and unequivocally.

If religion is seen as a matter of objective truth, in my view, as in that of many others from very different backgrounds, the choice came down to one of Catholicism or atheism. Other Christian bodies were relics of bygone issues in the history of the church that should now be resolved and put behind us. Jews and Muslims belonged to the same historic intervention of divine revelation. In the long run they too must find it in its fullest form. As for Buddhism and Hinduism, they represented precious discoveries of ways of self-purification that in their highest forms could be incorporated among the diverse traditions of Christian spirituality, some of which they closely resembled. Especially in its more ecumenical forms, Catholic Christianity did seem to offer the possibility of a genuinely catholic, open, dynamic account of the divine purpose focused ultimately on eternal life. What it promised was unique and wonderful. But could it deliver?

In taking this position I put myself in the hands of the church. I was gambling on its living up to its own claims. At the same time I committed myself to be truthful in judging whether or not it did so. Not that I doubted the outcome, but I recognised that only by being honest with myself could I hope to convince others. The required judgment was deeply problematical. Obviously, throughout its history the official church had failed repeatedly when judged by the standards of the gospels. There were excuses, but when did the excuses run out? There were innumerable failures, but they seemed never to be final. The institution picked itself up and promised renewal. When did those promises lose credibility? Nobody can pretend to be an impartial judge in such matters. There is no neutral ground on which to stand, no systematic procedure for arriving at a verdict, no decisive test. For some years to come I felt sufficiently strong in my faith to give the church the benefit of the doubt. I became proficient in the art of displaying the weaknesses of so many of the arguments of the opposition. Above all, I was very conscious of the danger of judging the church according to my personal preferences. The point of religion was that it bound one to conform to what it demanded. That was what was special about religion as opposed to poetry and other expressions of feeling for what lies beyond the banality of everyday routine.

The power of religion lies in its being full of enactments, ceremonies and other ways of interconnecting events in complex concrete social realities. Enactments are a pervasive feature of human life, raising mere physical activity to new levels of significance. The least controversial examples are serious sports. Kicking a leather ball through a pair of posts is, in the appropriate context, scoring a goal. That in turn can be a matter of a team winning or losing not just a game but a competition in which the hopes and fears, even the identities and self-perceptions of millions of fans are strongly involved. Challenged with treating football as a matter of life and death an English coach famously replied: 'No, it's much more important than that!' He had a point. Mere survival is not in itself of much importance. What gives life importance is what we do with it. Football is one of the things that contribute to the meanings of their lives for many people. It elevates a seemingly trivial activity into a living social drama, an enactment that constitutes an order of meaning that celebrates skill, courage, strength, cooperation and other such admirable and satisfying human characteristics. Such involvement transforms the merely physical into a higher, more specifically human reality, not just for the performers, but for those who identify with them.

Again, there are cultures that are extremely paranoid, in which people are dominated by fear of the numerous ways in which others may harm them, especially various forms of magic ritual. These people believe in magic because it is an integral part of their lives, enacted and re-enacted in ritual and incorporated in a host of precautions against it. They maintain these beliefs because although to us they seem to make life miserable, to the believers all this plotting and counter-plotting makes life much more interesting than just a boring routine of providing for one's daily needs. Getting them to change their way of life willingly involves involving them practically in more satisfactory ways of giving life meaning. Enactments and practices that have a central role in a form of life are not very vulnerable to arguments that the factual assumptions that underpin them are false, as long as that form of life retains its living significance.

At this stage in my life, while I was involved with philosophy as an insider, my primary involvement continued to be with my religion and specifically with my functions as a priest of the church. The philosophical enterprise was important, and in a way independent of, but in no way contrary to the religious one, which remained more important precisely because it invoked a supernatural power of supreme importance. Being involved daily in re-enacting the sacrifice of the son of God and the sacraments that channelled transforming grace into the souls of those who worshipped him, put philosophical arguments into a very secondary role.

Back Home

I returned to Sydney in mid 1954 on one of the last voyages of the venerable P&O liner *Strathnaver,* much more at ease now than on the voyage out. After a few months as a curate in Dulwich Hill, I was appointed to teach philosophy at my old seminary, St Columba's College, Springwood, in the Blue Mountains, seventy kilometres west of Sydney. I struggled uneasily with the task. On the one hand I had to provide students with the vocabulary and theses they needed to progress through the rest of their professional training. On the other I felt compelled to introduce them to a more sophisticated idea of philosophy. I was not very successful. My lectures floundered, though nobody seemed to mind very much. I was very isolated. My colleagues were a likeable bunch of men, but with hardly any interest in intellectual issues. There was no library of any use to which I had access. I had few contacts outside of the college. My one day off was spent mainly in visiting my parents at Manly and taking in the odd movie. My recreation at Springwood consisted in bushwalking and attempting to restore an old prewar Mercedes 320 Saloon.

Frustrating though it was, I was not unhappy. I spent a lot of time mastering the later works of Wittgenstein as they became available through the translations of Elizabeth Anscombe and others. It was an unsettling experience to take seriously Wittgenstein's challenge to the basic assumptions of the philosophical enterprise in virtually all its forms. It became increasingly clear to me that even many who professed great admiration for his work did not fully appreciate how radical a critique it offered of what philosophers thought they were doing. This is a matter to which we shall have to return later in the narrative.

Meanwhile, I retained the sense that the church was on the move. In particular, the number of candidates for the priesthood continued to grow. Already St Patrick's College Manly had been substantially extended and now I became involved in plans to double the capacity of St Columba's. Moreover, the quality of the candidates seemed to be improving. They seemed more open-minded. During this time Roger Pryke, whom I had come to know as a student a few years his senior in the seminary was appointed parish priest of Camperdown and chaplain to Catholic students at Sydney University. Roger soon built up a small but lively community of students around new pastoral and liturgical practices and an active engagement with other university movements. He began to draw me into his orbit.

My years at Springwood coincided with the Cold War taking its final shape as the United States and the Soviet Union entered into the arms race that was to build up arsenals of intercontinental missiles with nuclear warheads sufficient to destroy almost all human life. As virtually everybody conceded, that our world depended on MAD, mutually assured destruction, continuing to deter both the superpowers from using their power was indeed mad. I came to the conclusion that the only remedy for the disease of war was to destroy the power of nation states. At this stage of my thinking I put my hopes in pacifist civil disobedience. If the overwhelming majority of people in every nation refused to cooperate in any way with the use of violence against other nations, even in self-defence, war could be stopped completely and finally. Such a transformation would require organisation and strong and persistent leadership, which only the world's great religious organisations could give. It would probably also require courage on the part of some nations to commit themselves to unilateral disarmament, relying on shame to force others to follow suit.

The idea was not as unrealistic as it sounds. Later in the century, beginning in Latin America and Southern Europe military dictatorships were to crumble one after another until the Soviet Union itself finally disintegrated. In this whole development the root cause was that the oppressors lost their nerve, running out of rationalisations for the failings of their regimes and not knowing what to do about it. Oppression is more vulnerable than it seems. On the other hand, it is too much to expect very myopic and traditionalist bodies such as religious organisations to rise to the challenge of outlawing war. More fundamentally, the problem of appropriate forms of social authority called for a more comprehensive answer than a narrowly focused critique of the power of states. The anarchist response that assumes that, once freed from fear of the state, people will find spontaneously ways of organising the things that need deliberate organisation, is too simplistic. I continued to think about the problem throughout the rest of my life.

A couple of days after the first satellite, Sputnik, was launched by the Russians in 1957, some of the staff of the seminary, including me, were walking in the grounds with Cardinal Gilroy. Somebody pointed to a light in the sky, saying it was probably Sputnik. Gilroy turned on him indignantly, saying that it was just another piece of lying propaganda. Gilroy's outburst was a salutary reminder of the capacity of authorities to believe only what they wanted to believe, secure in the knowledge that nobody dared contradict them. It did not matter that they knew that others disagreed as long as they didn't say so. Power was what mattered. What the powerful did not understand was how they deluded themselves. Acton was right. Power corrupts.

Sputnik was just one more instance of the ways in which science-based technology was transforming the world. Soon there would be thousands of satellites and the day would come when even poor kids in African slums possessed mobile phones, capable, courtesy of satellites, of reaching people almost anywhere in the world. Men would land on the moon and people everywhere would watch them arrive and return. Already in 1953 Crick and Watson would track down the genetic code to DNA, opening up the possibility of controlling the basic structures of all living things. Increasingly undreamt of possibilities were opening up, exploiting processes that we could not even have imagined to be possible. All these new possibilities had potential for good and for evil that posed ever more insistently the problem of control, of reliable decision-making and humane but effective implementation. Hard, critical, realistic thinking was becoming daily more important. Traditional nostrums could no longer cope with our problems.

At a more local level I became increasingly concerned about the racism of White Australia, which remained one of our dominant myths, governing both immigration law and the treatment of Aboriginal people. The Anglo-centred assumptions of prewar Australians had been abandoned postwar under the slogan 'Populate or Perish', which still harked back to old fears of 'The Yellow Peril'. But an Australia that had to live in an Asian context could not continue to offer all Asians a standing and gratuitous insult. Slowly attitudes began to change. Chinese restaurants sprouted everywhere and people began to relate to Chinese communities in Singapore and

Hong Kong as equals. In the case of the Aboriginal peoples things moved more slowly. We had a bad conscience about our treatment of them that was guiltily suppressed. We could not admit to ourselves or anybody else that we had taken these lands by force and treated the native inhabitants abominably. I recall a weary farmer in the midst of a drought saying: 'It's a bastard of a country. We ought to give it back to the abos!' All the themes of white supremacy were there, the assumption of superiority, the guilt, the unwillingness to face the problems. The church did almost nothing about it.

If you ask how I could be so critical of the church, the seminary and of Australian society and yet remain reasonably content with my situation, the answer is that I really did have a strong trust in God's providence, in the social processes of advancing knowledge and in the basic capacity of Australian society to reform itself. I always counted my blessings, making the best of what my situation offered. While I tried to be rigorously critical, I got no joy out of any feeling that I understood things better than others. Things were too complicated for that. I was not by temperament an activist but a thinker who was wary of naive enthusiasm and of pushing others around. I believed that a vocation comes from God, and that he would send the opportunity to do whatever he wanted me to do. I waited patiently and the opportunity came.

St John's

In the latter half of 1958, in the fourth year of my life at Springwood, Archbishop James Carroll, auxiliary bishop to Cardinal Gilroy, told me that he and others were anxious to see a priest of the archdiocese appointed to the rectorship of St John's College within the University of Sydney, a post that had become vacant with the death of Father John Thompson, who was a member of the Vincentian order. The appointment was in the hands of the fellows of the College Council, who were said to be anxious to interest the archdiocese in supporting the college much more strongly than it had in the past. All the other

Catholic residential colleges in the Australian universities were at that time in the hands of members of the Society of Jesus, which represented the pinnacle of Catholic intellectual life. Gilroy and Carroll wanted to keep the Jesuits out, particularly because many of them were closely associated with the political machinations of Catholic Action.

I commended myself to the electors as a quiet, scholarly, presentable candidate who was in good standing with the archdiocese. So they preferred me to the other main candidate, Roger Pryke, who was seen as too much a stirrer to be a sound college man and in danger of antagonising rather than coopting the hierarchy. Taking up my post late in 1958, entirely without experience of the university and its colleges, I was most fortunate in having many people who rallied to help me, notably my colleague, Roger Pryke, the very able Mother Yvonne Swift, Principal of the sister college of Sancta Sophia next door, Doreen Langley, Principal of the Women's College and the Principal of St Andrew's, the Presbyterian College, the Reverend Alan Dougan. I also made firm friends among the former students of the college.

The university residential colleges were an odd Victorian compromise. The ostensible aim was to reproduce in the colonies institutions that would follow as closely as possible the model of the ancient universities. Oxford and Cambridge were still under the control of the clergy of the established church and saw as their prime function the preservation of the classical culture of Christian tradition. In the colonies there was no established church and little high culture. What the colonies wanted were well-educated professionals and administrators. The churches were horrified at the prospect of a purely secular university. So it was agreed that each of the major denominations should be allowed to erect its own college within the university to provide residence for its adherents and to give recognised courses in such matters as theology and modern history. However, the colleges had no say in the policies of the university and there was no structure through which their courses might be integrated into its degree structures. The teaching role was never put into practice. The colleges functioned mainly as hostels for country students and a few wealthier students who imitated the mores of Oxbridge undergraduates. Where they served their members well was in providing a network of contacts in the professions that assisted many of them to the top ranks. The collegians saw themselves as an elite, even if they were not highly regarded by other undergraduates, who dismissed them as a boring, ultraconservative clique.

I set myself to making the college a living Catholic presence in the university, meeting the expectations people tended to place on it, encouraging Catholic professional bodies and groups of Catholic academics to hold meetings and seminars there and reaching out to other bodies, such as the NSW Society for Immigration Reform, the Blake Prize for Religious Art and various academic associations to exploit its impressive public spaces and facilities. Wherever possible I took an active part in these events. At the same time I sought to build up a high table of resident tutors in the hope of improving the academic life of the students and making the college a place where important figures in the life of the university were happy to come and dine. I encouraged the studious and attempted to discourage the bibulous and rowdy among the students.

The college building was a Taj Mahal, a monument to a dead Romantic past, ill-adapted to its present role. As designed by the great Wardell its tower was to be higher than that of the central university quadrangle and everything about its public spaces was on the grand scale, leaving very little for the accommodation of students. The revenue from their fees was chronically inadequate to the costs of maintaining a building of crumbling sandstone, disintegrating slate and interior lathe and plaster walls and ceilings, now over a hundred years old, with antiquated furnishings and equipment. Fortunately for everybody, I was able to rely on the assistance in these matters of an able Vice-Rector, Ron Hine, and a wonderful household administrator, Pat Carroll. They worked for a pittance, enjoying the challenge.

Finally, when the Menzies government faced up to the task of expanding Australia's universities to meet the demands of the postwar world, the archtraditionalist himself insisted that the expansion should include substantial grants to the traditional colleges. So I was required to preside over a building program that involved a major reconstruction of a good deal of the original building and additions that more than doubled the number of residents. The first of the new wings was named after Menzies, who opened it in style. Against my modernist tastes, it was faced with sandstone at great cost. Adding to the disaster, the builder insisted in cleaning the stonework with muriatic acid, leaving it an ugly orange colour to the present day, still clashing with the delicate complexities of colour and texture of the sandstone original.

One gratifying result of my appointment to St John's was that I inherited from my predecessor the post of national chaplain to the Society of St Vincent de Paul. The Vinnies had been founded in Paris in the 1830s by a young Catholic intellectual, a republican and a democrat, named Frederic Ozanam (1813–1853), responding to taunts from followers of Saint Simon that the church was doing nothing to alleviate the sufferings of the poor. The members of the society joined together to visit the poor in their own homes, rather than make them come as clients to an institution, and do what they could to meet the specific needs of the people they met. It was a firm principle of the Society that the title of people to assistance was need alone, not desert or any religious, political or societal qualification. The Society enjoyed an excellent reputation for fidelity to its principles and for the effectiveness of its work.

The Vinnies were a genuinely lay organisation, in no way a tool of the hierarchy, and the role of the chaplain was to give theological guidance and motivation. That was not as simple as it sounds. Some theologians were inclined to insist that the fundamental point of the society was to offer its members a means of acquiring merit in the sight of God, by doing God's will. They feared that its members might develop a 'merely humanitarian' outlook. At its worst this orientation could come across as not very different from that of people who engaged in charitable works to enhance their social standing. Both treated the poor as ultimately just means to their own ends. On the other hand, it was important for helpers to keep a certain distance from those they tried to help, discouraging emotional involvement, unrealistic expectations and dependency. Charity is not an adequate answer to social problems, much less people's personal problems. The Society has always been conscious of its limitations and has consistently supported the need for government programs to remedy the causes of poverty and for professional casework.

Another side effect of my being at St John's was that I became involved with the Blake Prize for Religious Art. I had always been strongly interested in painting. Even at Maynooth I managed to scrape together the money to buy a minor work of Charles Lamb. I was coopted by Michael Scott SJ, Rector of Newman College in Melbourne University and one of the founders of the prize, and Alan Dougan, who was an amateur painter with many artist friends. I was a judge on several occasions and became chair of the committee at a critical time, when it faced threats of extinction. The people who had endowed the prize were deeply dissatisfied with the entries that had won and drawn most attention in recent years. They threatened to withdraw their support. At the same time the gallery at the old department store, Mark Foys, became unavailable. Fortunately, I managed to negotiate an arrangement with the Commonwealth Bank to use their magnificent banking chamber in Martin Place, prompting predictable quips about God and Mammon. Somehow the donors were pacified and the prize flourished in its new surroundings.

I believed very firmly that the arts can enlarge our horizons in ways that neither science nor philosophy nor any set of true propositions can, but I was never very comfortable with the idea of religious art, or, at a later stage, political art. Explicit religious references were neither necessary nor sufficient to make a painting religious. Many a Renaissance Madonna was obviously secular while some rural landscapes had as distinctive a religious dimension as a poem of Gerard Manley Hopkins. Abstract painting often succeeded in expressing strong emotions, which might relate to a religious context. But for all their power it seemed that the religious context had to be supplied from outside the painting, perhaps by the way in which it was placed in a church or religious institution. I was happy to see the Blake prize flourish, because the religious iconography of the times was so disastrous, feebly didactic, sickly sentimental and commercially facile. It needed the shock of the new.

During this period I came into conflict with the diocesan authorities over some of my publicly expressed views on disputed questions. I accepted that as an official of the church I was committed to standing up for its teaching in public, but that I was perfectly entitled to express views that, although defensible as within the bounds of orthodoxy, were at variance with the views of my immediate superiors. I argued that, although abortion was morally unacceptable, it should not be a crime. The law ought not enforce every moral principle or pretend to protect the innocent in every situation. The view that an unviable foetus is not fully human is held seriously by responsible people. The church should not push the state to override their views.

In treating premarital sex in sermons in the college chapel I left no doubt that it was morally wrong, but I went on to add that if one is doing wrong one still has an obligation to minimise the harm that might result from one's actions. If one engaged in premarital coitus one should take effective precautions against conception. I was well aware that conservative theologians took the view that to use contraception was to add the sin of committing an unnatural act to the sin of unjustified sexual intercourse. The line must be held.

The only way of avoiding undesirable pregnancies is abstinence. I was called on to defend myself, but somehow managed to escape punishment. I came to realise that the dogmatic view of the 'true nature' of sex acts was indefensible. It was only gradually, however, that I came to abandon all the baggage that came with it, especially in regard to homosexuality. Unfortunately, this absurd rigidity persists. The pope continues to condemn the use of condoms to halt the spread of AIDS and even to endorse the demonstrably false claim that they are ineffective.

Teaching Philosophy

It so happened that my arrival at the university coincided with the departure of Professor John Anderson, who since 1927, the year of my birth, had been the most prominent figure in the intellectual life of Sydney. In those days, especially in the smaller Arts departments that were not devoted to equipping school teachers, the professor was the department. If there were other members involved in teaching, they were considered his assistants. Anderson was a forthright atheist and in his early days a communist sympathiser. His pronouncements on public affairs resulted in strong pressure on the Senate of the university to bring him to heel; this he met with scathing counterattacks, demanding to be told how he could be required to teach what he knew to be nonsense. The Senate sought to deal with the situation by setting up a department of mental and moral philosophy to which they appointed Alan Stout, son of GF Stout, a noted philosophical psychologist. Alan Stout got on well with Anderson. Although moderately agnostic and a significant moral philosopher, he was not the counter to Anderson that the churches had hoped for. When there were further rumblings seeking to bring the teaching of philosophy into a mode more acceptable to the churches, I weighed in on the side of academic freedom.

As the cynical would have it, my reward was that in 1960 Stout and John Mackie, Anderson's successor, appointed me to a part-time lectureship in philosophy. From that time onwards the philosophy department, now once again a single department, but with a very varied and rapidly expanding staff, became one of the two centres of the ellipse of my life. I took a very active role in seminars and informal discussions, working hard at keeping up with new developments. Not a lot of that discussion was explicitly concerned with religion and I never taught a course on a religious topic, though I did pride myself on being able to answer most of the objections that were thrown up against the existence of God. The standard objection, set out precisely and lucidly by Mackie in a well-known article, was that at least some evils, especially moral evils, were contingent. It was incompatible with God's moral perfection and omnipotence to permit, let alone sustain such evils. God could have created a better world. I developed the response: how do you know he hasn't? Perhaps he has created a whole spectrum of worlds, exemplifying different possibilities. We happen to be part of this one and have to make the most of the opportunities it offers. Are you saying that either the moral or the physical evil in this world is such that it would be better for it not to exist? That seems excessively puritanical or excessively pessimistic.

Such a reply was fairly typical of my philosophical style. As my colleague David Stove put it: 'I move known pieces around the board, but you are always trying to change the pieces and even the rules of the game.' Stove was understandably suspicious of such strategies. In the case in point, the suggestion that the infinitely powerful and infinitely intelligent creator might find it interesting to create many worlds invites the suggestion that God created all possible worlds. But that, as the great Jewish philosopher, Baruch Spinoza saw, leads to the collapse of any distinction between God and Nature, conceived as the inevitable unfolding of all the infinite varieties of being. If you want to allow many possibilities, but not others, what rationale can you give for drawing a line between the acceptable and the unacceptable? In discussing such matters it was wonderful to be among people who were interested in exploring arguments and suggestions without too many preconditions.

The first task to which I was assigned was to deliver lectures along with other staff in the first-year logic program, which dated from Anderson's days and was deeply infected with his dogmatism. One of the foundations of Anderson's system was an idiosyncratic metaphysical interpretation of traditional syllogistic logic as revealing the structure of all reality. Contemporary logic was dismissed out of hand. The result was a course that was as embarrassing as the worst constructions of Roman Thomism. Anderson could be an acute critic of other people's dogmas, but tended to represent those criticisms as embodying sweeping universal principles. Each of those principles was supposed to guard against a specific fallacy to which almost everybody else succumbed at some point or other. The spirit of the enterprise was in some respects like that of Ludwig Wittgenstein's *Tractatus Logico-Philosophicus,* erecting criteria of clarity and declaring that everything that can be said can be said clearly. What could not be said clearly could not be said at all. They differed diametrically in the significance of the boundary. Wittgenstein thought that everything of importance in human life lay outside the boundaries of what can be said. Anderson thought that what lay beyond his boundary was error and illusion. That brash, no-nonsense dogmatism was very attractive to a 'tough-minded', irreverent Australian self-image, and its ethos became an important strand of Sydney's *avant garde.* Unfortunately, it flourished in isolation and Anderson's institutional monopoly of philosophy in Sydney.

Wittgenstein came to abandon the idea that there was a single utterly clear and unquestionable structure underlying all language, insisting on the irreducible variety of forms of language and their dependence as 'language games' on the specific limits and social contexts of their practical applicability. Some of his early disciples systematised this insight in the doctrine that 'the meaning of a statement is the method by which it can be verified'. But verificationism, often called logical positivism, was too restrictive, even as an account of the languages of the physical sciences. Physicists were not just correlating pointer readings on certain instruments. The Oxford philosophers who concentrated on the analysis of ordinary language were nearer the mark, though they were often too complacent about assuming that there was such a thing as *the* concept, say, of mind, which was embodied in their particular dialect of English.

Given the complexity of my various commitments and my anxiety to keep up with developments in a variety of fields, I failed to carve out for myself a particular network of contacts in any special field or to develop papers for publication from discussion papers delivered to seminars or conferences. It was not only a question of time or of dispersed interests. My bent was, as has been said, to attempt to upset the assumptions underlying the way questions and problems were stated and debated. I agreed strongly with Wittgenstein's view that most philosophical problems arose from various misuses of language, but that no systematic account of language was likely to be of use in countering them, since such accounts typically involve just the sort of oversimplifications they are supposed to counter. The traditional philosophical demand for a comprehensive view of ultimate reality is a disease for which there is no final cure.

Religion and Disappointment

The Second Vatican Council in the 1960s marked the high point of my hopes for the church. By contrast with the First Vatican Council, which had met in 1870 to signal the church's defiance of the modern world and to impose an ever stricter discipline on its members, the new council, under the leadership of Pope John XXIII, set out to define a new approach to the relations of the church to other religions and to the rapidly changing world. Abandoning the traditional view that the prime duty of the state was to maintain the true faith and suppress error wherever that was possible without causing worse evils, the council proclaimed the doctrine of freedom of conscience in all circumstances. It embraced the view that other religions were to be treated with respect, and that dialogue with them could be salutary for all concerned. It introduced a vernacular, participatory liturgy in which the priest functioned as leader of the congregation rather than as an epiphany of the godhead. There was even a substantial move to abandon the rigorous condemnation of 'artificial contraception'. Many disciplinary regulations were relaxed, including the iconic abstinence from meat on Fridays.

There were many rearguard actions by the traditionalists during the council, but at the time it seemed that their few successes were temporary, and that the course towards the future was firmly set. It turned out otherwise. While many of the more superficial changes remained in place, the Vatican soon reverted to its authoritarian ways. Discussion of matters of sexual ethics in particular was thoroughly suppressed and liberal theologians removed from teaching wherever possible. It was crystal clear that, having declared itself infallible, the papacy was deeply afraid of giving the appearance of admitting it had been wrong on a matter of such great concern to almost everybody as sexual ethics. It made an enormous, almost fatal, mistake. Not only did it cause great disappointment, but it set in train a radical change of attitude to authority in the church. As one prominent priest was to sum up the outcome, 'We are all Protestants now.' Pious Catholics came to believe what they personally felt was right, not what the authorities told them. Like most Protestants, they identified with the core traditions and practices of their community, but felt free to disagree with authorities that were seen as insensitive and inflexible.

That adaptation was easy enough for the laity, but it posed acute problems for many priests, including me, who felt that they could no longer represent officially an authority that they saw as deeply discredited. Very many left the ministry and vocations to the priesthood dried up almost overnight, falling to a tenth of what they had been a few years before. Within a few years both the seminaries in Sydney were closed completely and permanently. Makeshift arrangements were improvised to cater for the few vocations that continued to come. Among those who remained in the ministry many no longer accepted the role of mouthpieces of authority, seeing themselves rather as servants of their parishioners. They were often confident that ultimately the church would change and struggled to change it, battling against authoritarianism at great cost to themselves. Even forty years later, vocations to the priesthood have not recovered.

For me the problem cut much deeper. The church had failed the crucial test. It was no longer possible to see it as the vehicle of divine revelation. The whole basis of my religion had collapsed. In my view the very existence of a personal god was plausible only if that god revealed itself in the world and the only plausible candidate for the revelation had now discredited itself. Others might want to save what they could from the wreckage, keeping up Christian traditions and values in the community of those who continued to find liturgical and other practices important for their sense of identity and commitment. Many people were very dependent on seeing their lives as the unfolding of a benign providence in which they could trust. It would be arrogant and destructive to attempt to disillusion them simply because one thought that both the metaphysical and historical bases of such a belief were invalid. But one could not continue to pretend that Catholicism, or even theism, was a set of truths that commanded assent.

Conservative traditionalists, I knew, would see my position as incoherent. I admitted that a divine revelation could not be expected to conform to what passed as common sense. So it needed an authority to proclaim and define it. But as soon as it exercised that authority in ways I and others influenced by secular humanism did not like, I rejected it as untrue to itself. My reply was that the church itself in solemn council had recognised that the authoritarian practices of the past had to be superseded, but that it had shown itself incapable of keeping its promise. Others, of a more liberal persuasion, felt sure that the church would change, as it had, usually unconsciously, but often with dubious rationalisations, so often changed in the past. I replied that they were probably right. The Vatican continued to proclaim its conversion to ecumenism while acting in ways that made a mockery of it. But in the long run it might be forced to live up to its pretensions. It might even catch up with the humanists, thus emphasising once again its own failure to lead and inspire.

Of course, religion is not a search for propositional truths. The point of prayer in any account is its effects on us, and these are independent of whether or not there is a personal god whom we may address. Still, if one does not believe in such a god, but only in some vaguely numinous ultimate reality, it surely makes a difference to one's prayer. Again, it may be objected that we should be cautious about commonsense in this context. Religious faith is the ultimate commitment. Prayer to an ultimately unknowable god is not like posting an incompletely addressed letter that is doomed to end up in the dead letter office. Rather it is a way of enacting a basic orientation in our values and attitudes. The question remains whether or not the values and attitudes involved are or are not appropriate to our situation.

The movement to communal worship revealed the limitations of ceremony as re-enactment in contemporary social contexts, limitations that had shown themselves in other earlier times in the fissiparous histories of sects. Congregations that strove to achieve a high degree of identification with a specific sacred focus inevitably needed a very specific iconography, a distinctive rhetoric and strong norms of conduct and aspiration. In a fluid and secular society such congregations tended to alienate those adherents who found that iconography unappealing, the rhetoric inflated and the moralism simplistic. Such people found it easy to drift away from the congregation, sometimes to another congregation, but more often, losing contact with any lively religious community. It was much easier to continue religious practice through attendance at the formalised, hieratic worship of ecclesiastical tradition which was much less prescriptive in its emotional demands on the worshipper. In either case in most contemporary societies religion was no longer a major social reality, even where most individuals professed some residual religious commitment.

Many still argued that the theistic hypothesis had not been refuted, and that even as a heuristic framework it still had a place among possible ways of making sense of our world. Even militant atheists like Richard Dawkins, while insisting that evolution by random mutations and natural selection was in reality a completely undirected, non-teleological process, found themselves using purposive models to spell out how it worked in practice. They spoke of the strategies that 'selfish' genes used to reproduce themselves using analyses derived from economic theory to develop models of their roles. One could not rule out a priori that, even if everything that happens is a matter of chance and necessity, it may still be useful to look at history as if it were the unfolding of purposive action, provided one is not dogmatic about it.[1]

---

1 The use of intentional models to elucidate non-intentional processes is not without its dangers. If for the gene an organism is just a way of making more genes, from the organism's point of view the gene is simply its way of making more organisms. But control of the process belongs to neither. The environment is what determines which organisms and genes survive, and at least in this respect it seems unlikely that intentional models are relevant. Even those who insist that the earth is a self-regulating system, Gaia, believe that it does not 'care' what happens to particular sets of organisms or genes. In any case it is not a closed system and the climate on which life depends has certainly been modified in the past by incursions from outer space and internal changes in the earth over which Gaia has no control.

The 'selfish gene' model tends to insist that it is individual genes that are 'selected' by natural selection, eliding the fact that genes face the task of reproduction as genomes, the configurations reproduced as wholes by organisms. In that process many a dysfunctional gene rides on the community of functional genes which shelters it. Insisting on finding an adaptive advantage for individual genes too

Still I did not think that traditional models of purpose were likely to be of use. In the case of evolutionary theory the model that analysed the dynamics of the process in terms of strategies could be translated without loss of content into language that made no reference to choices or intentions. But that is not the case with the processes of history. Hegel spoke of 'the cunning of Reason' in history, but even he would admit that it was a metaphor that needed judicious interpretation and qualification. The unpredictable horrors of the twentieth century had destroyed the plausibility of any claims to find a providential or teleological pattern in history. One could not exclude the possibility that personifying historical agencies might be useful, if used with due caution. Such models have an advantage over more mechanistic models in highlighting choice, which in turn accommodates the roles of contingency and of alternative possibilities in understanding historical developments. But that use of personification is very different from its religious uses. Religion is binding, overriding.

---

easily results in the fabrication of 'just so' stories that are pure speculation. Things are much more complex than that.

There is a curious parallel between religious enthusiasts who insist on reading a providential explanation into every event and those evolutionists who find a selective advantage in every surviving mutation. Both give the illusion of being able to find a purpose in everything, ignoring the complex roles of chance. They compete in speculation rather than science, seeking to dominate the imagery that gives shape to people's attitudes.

There is no more difficulty in supposing that a divine providence rules a Darwinian world than any other sort of world. The challenge of evolutionary theory is that it shows that it is not necessary to appeal to divine intervention to explain the emergence of life. We don't need that hypothesis for that or any other explanatory purpose. Moreover, in the absence of any clear knowledge of divine purposes, appeal to them explains nothing. 'Intelligent Design' is intellectually vacuous.

However, we live in imagination rather than knowledge and it may stimulate imagination, as its proponents hope, though I fear it is more likely to constrain it.

Adjusting to the Loss of Faith

I did not think that religions like Christianity and Islam could be freed from their dogmatic matrix. The role of official interpreter of revealed truth is an irresistible temptation to authoritarianism. Not content with proclaiming their gospel, religious authorities seek to enforce its injunctions and demonise dissent. More fundamentally, looking for understanding in terms of an originating agent's choices tended to be backward-looking and restrictive. The purposes we attribute to the originator are inevitably drawn from the past and limited to the possibilities that can be envisaged in terms of the past. We have to face the fact that we cannot realistically claim to know where we are likely to go, because we do not know what possibilities the numerous changes that we cannot anticipate are opening up to us. All our institutions, rules and practices are the product of a social evolution that, as far as we can see, works in much the same undirected way as organic evolution. Deviations from existing norms in every aspect of life occur for a variety of reasons. Some become more frequent and displace old norms of belief and practice, but most inevitably die out. It is all too complex and too much a matter of coincidences and extraneous factors intruding on, and even changing permanently, the workings of functional systems, to be conceived as directed by a single purpose. What survives, what makes progress possible, is what succeeds in adapting to changing circumstances. Dogmatism stifles adaptation. Insisting that we conform to patterns and purposes set in the past, shuts out constructive change.

Where intelligent, controlling, desiring beings are involved adaptation cannot be left to chance. We have our values, our needs and our aspirations and as individuals and as groups we look for ways of changing our world to accord with them. Most of that striving takes place in very limited and often transitory contexts, adapting in limited ways to particular circumstances. A minority, however, are always looking to wider contexts and for systematic changes. When they are dogmatic and addicted to compulsion such minorities are clearly dangerous, especially because implementing their views usually involves forcing those who do not agree to conform to the plan. Conceiving whole societies on the model of either natural organisations like plants or social organisations like corporations or armies may be useful as long as we remain conscious of the limitations of such models. Or, more precisely, we have to acknowledge that we are inevitably ignorant of most of those limitations and completely unable to quantify them or gauge their importance.

What, then was I to make of the content of my abandoned faith? Its key promise had been that of eternal blissful fulfilment. I had always regarded that promise as conceptually and imaginatively mysterious, not at all something one might expect or desire or even hope for. While most people in most cultures had expected some kind of life after death, few had regarded the prospect with much enthusiasm. A shadowy underworld, a perilous reincarnation or a haunted ghostly existence had been the sorts of thing that people were inclined to expect. As we came to think of ourselves in more naturalistic terms we became more inclined to accept that we survive death only in the memories of other people and the legacies we leave behind. The idea of a state of eternal happiness involving the resurrection of our bodies was as unexpected and challenging a doctrine as those of the trinity and the incarnation of God the son.

Because it was so mysterious it was difficult to see our earthly lives as a preparation for heaven. That preparation reduced to the performance of religious and moral observances that seemed at best very shadowy anticipations of the life to come. In practice these observances were presented as the price we paid under God's covenant with us for admission to the heavenly kingdom. So Pascal argued that what was offered us was of infinite value and that it was worth gambling any finite amount on attaining it, even if the odds of its being available to us were not high. For many faith was such a gamble, but without some sound assurance of the credibility of such an implausible message the promise was worthless. One had to accept that there was no good reason to expect to survive death. The loss was not a deprivation of something I felt I needed, but of something I had accepted as one of the mysteries of revealed religion.

Another key element in the Christian view of our situation was the doctrine of original sin, explicated as a primordial rejection of divine authority that resulted in a moral corruption infecting all human beings and rendering them incapable of the happiness God had prepared for them. It was from this unhappy condition that the incarnation, death and resurrection of the son of God would rescue them. Whatever one might think about this account of our situation, the empirical evidence for the view that there was something radically wrong with the way in which human beings so often treated each other had always seemed to me overwhelming. It seemed to call for a radical diagnosis. Certainly the rationalist expectation that scientific progress would inevitably go hand in hand with the development of a more rational morality had been decisively disappointed.

My very general and rather thin diagnosis of our problem was, however, still in the tradition of the Enlightenment. The problem was that most of our ways of resolving conflicts of interest in practice involved the exercise of power, credible threats to harm people if they failed to do what those who controlled superior resources demanded. Reliance on moral injunctions to restraint in the use of power was inadequate, because the exercise of power almost always corrupted the moral vision of those who wielded it and those who supported them, glorifying their objectives and proclaiming their beneficence. Even when mythical legitimations were debunked, rationalistic utilitarian arguments appealing to the long term good of all could be made to justify the most appalling treatment of those who stood in the way of the greater good.

The view that market exchanges provided *the* way in which people can resolve their differences without threats is illuminating, but simplistic. People do not agree to a market exchange unless each hopes to benefit from it. The trouble is that when it comes to selling their labour some groups are in a very different position from others. Those with abilities for which there is strong demand are free to accept or reject any particular bid for their services. Those in desperate need of a job with nothing special to recommend them are forced to accept whatever they are offered. Wealth, or the lack of it, is very powerful in assigning people to social positions by determining the options available to them. There are many ways in which markets fail to deliver what people need to live a decent life.

I concluded that what we need is a variety of social practices that can ensure that the various problems that we encounter can evoke appropriate responses, treating each problem according to its specific character. Abandoning both religious and philosophical dogmatism, I had joined the more pragmatic wing of the secular humanists. This focus was hardly a substitute for a religious commitment. It was both naturalistic and vague, though in time I did develop it into something more definite and with a particular moral dimension. The surprising fact was that I no longer felt the need for a religious commitment, and it seemed to me that relatively few other people were worried any longer by the secularisation of our culture. Humanism allowed the reflective appropriation of the poetry and sensibility of religions once they were shorn of pretentions to authority. All that was lost was the security provided by specious authority.

Religion had lost the halo that used to surround it. It no longer had any crucial social importance, however important it might be to some individuals. It was not, as was often claimed, that it had succumbed to crass materialism. People had come to think, like Luther, that human nature was not to be reformed by religious belief. Unlike Luther, they no longer felt the need for redemption or for eternal life. Whatever they might say, they acted as if this life alone mattered, but it was far from hopeless. The basic structure of our appetites might be hard-wired into our genes so that we could never escape them. The urge to gratify them could be destructive to individuals and societies, but people could be induced to gratify their appetites in sustainable and creative ways. The sort of redemption we needed was to be found in exploring those possibilities in all their technological, economic, cognitive, moral and aesthetic dimensions. What mattered was not what we were made of, but what we could make of what we were made of. Not conformity to preset standards, but setting ourselves higher, but more realistic, standards.

A lot of priests left the church, or at least the priesthood, about the same time as I did. Among those that stayed in the priesthood were some very admirable men. I had formed strong ties with Ted Kennedy when he was chaplain to students at Sydney University and I was still at St John's, in spite of our approaching our roles from quite different viewpoints. I was a philosopher, a theoretician concerned with the truth of abstract propositions. Ted was a poet, concerned with inspiration, vision and, above all, sensitivity to individual people, especially those who were suffering. Questions of literal truth, especially metaphysical questions, were to him largely irrelevant to his religious life. Religion was a powerful way of expressing effectively in ritual, story and action relationships and values that enriched the lives of many people by providing them with personal involvement in a living community.

Ted found his fulfilment in the community that he built up in the Aboriginal quarter of Redfern. He understood and responded to the culture and humanity of Aboriginal people, often at great cost to himself. He was a person of discriminating tastes, but his presbytery was often full of drunks sleeping off their excesses. He responded to Aboriginal assumptions that what any member of the community possessed was to be shared with anybody else who needed it. He knew everybody, would talk to them from within their perspectives and feelings and tried to protect them from those who wanted to force them to change. Ecclesiastical officialdom was very disturbed by his disregard of conventional propriety. When he died, worn out by his labours, they moved quickly to close down the community he had built and sustained.

Beyond Religion

I resisted defining myself negatively as an atheist, especially if that was understood as the proclamation that God is dead, so everything is permitted and human life is senseless. On the contrary, I thought that the great achievement of secular humanists over the past two centuries had been to free morality from legalistic casuistry and the negativity of 'thou shalt not', establishing a much more sensitive and demanding morality of concern for the feelings, interests and liberties of other human beings. The days when it seemed that only the threat of savage punishment in the present and hellfire hereafter could motivate most people to 'keep the commandments' were long gone. The revolutions in social and sexual morality that were shaking Western societies and abolishing so many prohibitions were indeed liberating, but their most important tendency was to demand that we should have consideration for what really matters, for the dignity and autonomy of all those affected by what we do. In this perspective the fundamental need for self-respect became a matter of the quality of one's personal relations, not just observance of some set of rules.

In moral practice, as in theoretical questions, it was important to break completely with foundationalism, especially in its negative aspect, the view that no claim to knowledge or moral principle that is not based on unquestionable foundations can be valid. What is not validated by such foundations should be dismissed as merely subjective opinion. On the contrary, knowledge of the natural world develops by refining rough data and vague ideas, introducing new and untried conceptions and wrestling with the problems they generate. Similarly, moral knowledge rests not on immutable imperatives but on exploring the demand for dignity and security in the satisfaction of our needs and the development of our individual and collective potential. The idea that for there to be meaning and worth in human life there must be some plan governing our destiny that is laid down authoritatively by some superior being is radically wrong, but the idea that in the absence of such a plan 'anything goes' is just as wrong.

Nature in its evolutionary process supplies us with raw materials and capacities that are open to continuing development in ways that we discover, sometimes by diligent enquiry, but more often by accident. Our history provides us with a heritage, but one that must continually be re-evaluated in the light of the problems that emerge from the largely uncontrollable process of change in which our lives are embedded. The results of our striving are inevitably a mixture of progress in some respects and loss in others. Only in retrospect can we recognise some important kinds of progress and some crippling kinds of failure. The resolution of a problem often demands that it be transformed into a different problem. The criteria of what constitutes a solution changes. We can never be entirely sure that such change is salutary in any particular case. That does not mean abandoning the search for evidence, but seeing it as a search for grounds that lead to mutual recognition and cooperation. A truth is rarely the whole truth.

A New Life

I set myself the task of articulating this emerging vision of the point of human life. Resigning the rectorship of St John's late in 1968 I took up a fulltime appointment in the philosophy department in 1969. I came to regard most of what occupied my time in my ten years at John's as wasted effort. The colleges were just student clubs, halls of residence that needed management, but were largely devoid of any academic or religious significance. In those years I learned a lot and made many friendships but achieved little. I gave myself a year in which to withdraw from any public role in the church and consider whether to break with it definitively. When I did so it was with little sense of loss, but no great feeling of liberation. My father was now dead and my mother accepted my decision, even if she could not understand it. The rest of my family and Catholic friends gave me credit for sincerity, even when they felt betrayed or at least abandoned. My defection made a substantial item of front page news in the *Sydney Morning Herald*, but soon was forgotten. I did not think there was much point in attacking the church. It no longer mattered very much.

By this time the sexual revolution was in full swing, but I was not drawn to sowing belated wild oats. My attitude to my own sexuality had been simple. Sex was natural and wonderful. But if one was to stand up in the pulpit and lay down the law to people in God's name, one owed them some pledge of good faith, particularly in view of the fact that as a priest one was assured of a comfortable economic and social status. One needed to sacrifice something substantial, and sex was the obvious, traditionally sanctioned way of doing that. I had always felt that my identity was a matter of being true to label. Other priests I knew and respected resented having labels pasted on them and strove to evade the demands placed upon them, often deeply torn between their vocational commitments and their need for love. For me, celibacy was not an arbitrary imposition. So it was not a source of resentment, but the price I had to pay for the sort of trust people accorded to me. My life in the church had not been a waste of time but an education that had led me to come to grips with some of the fundamental problems facing us. It had been a constructive experience, very limited and limiting in important respects, as every experience must be, but not a matter for regret.

As far as I could see, I had come through celibacy undamaged, but not without some deficiencies. I was unpractised in the arts of pleasing women on every level, from the simplest courtesies of courtship to the psychology and physiology of sex, and insensitive to the subtleties of romantic involvements. In so many ways I was a literal-minded intellectual, almost always a spectator rather than a participant in the games that constitute the bulk of most people's lives. Nobody came to me with the latest gossip. They assumed I was not interested and I never had anything to trade. I tried to avoid taking sides in the conflicts that arise out of the friction of social life. I told myself I saw the good in everybody, but at the cost, I came to fear, of blunting my sensitivity to the complexities of people's feelings and needs. But I did want to break out of my lonely shell and I looked forward to founding a family.

Looking among my acquaintance for a life companion, I courted Patricia Baillie, a vivacious, intellectually acute and aesthetically sensitive postgrad in the department. A divorcee with two children in primary school, she was a latecomer to university study with a refreshing combination of professional seriousness and fierce independence of mind and spirit. Unfortunately (fortunately?), she was appointed to a lectureship in Auckland, where she fell in love with a wild Irishman. Returning from a visit to Auckland, where this news broke, I turned my attention to an old acquaintance who had just returned to a lectureship in English after completing a PhD in London. I had become distantly aware of Margaret Harris when, in spite of being a lapsed Presbyterian, she held a resident tutorial position in Sancta Sophia College, the Catholic women's college next to St John's. Renewing acquaintance I found a partner whom I came quickly to admire and love for her unique qualities, which made up for some of my deficiencies. We achieved an attunement that has endured, in spite of a few bars of discord, to the present day.

Margaret's outstanding quality is the directness and appropriateness of her intuitions and her emotional reactions. Her spouse, by contrast, is not very perceptive and evolves his reactions only in a laborious process of mulling over events. Again, Margaret has a marvellous capacity to hold together all the strands of a practical problem while I am apt to lose sight of some important part of it in my fascination with other aspects of it. She is fifteen years younger than I and for some years suffered in the countless ways, not always appreciated by me, in which a male chauvinist academic context lacerated her self-esteem. Only late in life did she receive the recognition her varied contributions to the life of the university, and of scholarship more generally, deserved. Our investment in the genetic lottery and in our home life produced two talented and loveable daughters who continue to be close to us and provide vicarious satisfactions through their achievements.

4

PHILOSOPHY AND REAL LIFE

The philosophy department was sometimes seen as the Church of Reason. Many philosophers had a missionary sense of their social role in championing enlightenment against the forces of obscurantism. Within the church of reason there were deeply conflicting views and attitudes that hid behind a certain unanimity about certain slogans. Liberty was prized, but what constituted liberation and what was self-indulgence or self-deception was a matter of profound disagreements. Truth was supremely important, but what constituted a genuine search for truth was hotly contested. These differences were to erupt into severe conflict in the near future.

The main interests in the Sydney philosophy department at this time were David Armstrong's materialist theory of mind, which chimed in with other people's interests in philosophy of science, the pragmatism of Quine, philosophy of science and David Stove's work on induction. Somewhat on the fringe, Bill Ginnane and others worked on new approaches to ethics, while others took to the emerging field of philosophy of language. It was a lively and stimulating place to work, even if the dominant tendency was a somewhat simplistic scientism. According to this orientation what was real was what made a difference in the physical world, what had irreducible and independent causal properties. Rejecting the old empiricist view that causality was just a pattern of one type of event following regularly on another, causality was seen as a matter of forces and powers. What those were was a matter for science, not philosophy. It could help by defending a realist interpretation of scientific theories against sceptical or minimalist accounts. These sometimes infected scientists themselves, who would speak of a conclusion as 'being consistent with' a certain set of data, where a realist would say that the data strongly supported it.

Conflict became sharpest in explaining mental operations. According to the materialist theory of mind the brain was the mind. It had to be, because the only demonstrable causal factors in human behaviour were physical. Admittedly, mental phenomena are described in terms that are irreducibly different from those describing physical phenomena, but as a matter of fact they are describing the same things. This is not surprising. In all sorts of contexts we find complexes that have properties that do not belong to their components taken in isolation. Clouds do things that molecules of water cannot. Clocks tell the time, but their cogs and springs do not. The mind is not just the sum of a lot of physical bits and pieces, but a supremely complex and marvellous organism that harnesses the powers of its components in unique ways. Philosophy can't prove by conceptual analysis that this is so, but it can help understanding by removing certain erroneous conceptions of mind that stand in the way of seeing how it could be a particular sort of complex physical mechanism.

Some of these 'errors' were easily disposed of. For example, the old conception of mind as completely transparent to itself was no longer plausible in the light of modern psychology. Most mental activity was unconscious, and self-awareness depended on specific circuits in which the mind became self-conscious in specific ways as it monitored certain of its own activities. The argument that matter was bound down in space while the mind transcended space could not be sustained. Again, what the alleged freedom of the will came down to was the important fact that the mind could regulate many of its own actions according to its own feelings and rational calculations. It was not just a ball tossed around by external forces, but an organism capable of understanding and mastering a great deal of its environment. As physiologists and psychologists came to understand more about the workings of the brain it became ever clearer how particular mental occurrences and activities were located in particular parts and processes of the brain.

Much more difficult were two other problems. We readily enough accept that the objective correlates of what we experience as colour or sound are photons or air waves. It is much harder to accept that colour perceptions not only reside in the brain but are nothing more than states of brain cells. Even if colour, as distinct from its physical embodiment, has no causal properties, is that sufficient reason for denying it any distinct reality? Having causal properties is a strong claim to being accepted as real, but are we sure that nothing can be a really distinct entity without making a detectable difference in the physical world? It was difficult to see any argument on this issue that does not beg the question. However, it did seem clear that the phenomena of sensory experience had structural relations that were not explicable in terms of their physical correlatives, such as the ways in which colours, sounds, textures, tastes and smells harmonised or clashed with each other. These relationships were in a sense subjective, but not in the way likes and dislikes are subjective. Some prefer dry wine, others sweet, but both seem to be attending to the same qualitative characteristics.

A different problem concerned the 'intentionality' of conceptual thinking, very roughly, the way in which ideas have precise meanings, even when nothing corresponds to them in reality. A statement may be completely false but have just as precise a meaning as a true one. In fact, unless it has a clear meaning, not only is it impossible to know that is false, it cannot be false. We have to be able to talk of things that do not exist. On the other hand physical things can relate physically only to other things that do exist. So it looks as if physical relations could never explain conceptual meanings. On this issue many subtle and highly technical arguments could be advanced and

I was caught up in discussions of them which led me to question the way in which the problem was posed. The motivation behind the materialist theory of mind was to discredit the view, traditional in almost all prescientific cultures, that there are two distinct kinds of beings, material things and spirits, with quite different powers, both of which are causally active in the world. It was a motivation I was now inclined to share, but the materialist thesis rested on a suspiciously sweeping assumption about the boundaries of the real.

Materialists tend to concentrate on showing that the mind is the brain. But just as a computer functions as a processor of information only in virtue of the software that is fed into it and its connections with a network of sources of input, all coded in a meaningful, logically structured language, so the brain is just a lot of electrochemical interactions unless it is programmed to interconnect with natural and conventional sign systems that function as a social network. Sign relations are quite different from causal relations. That does not mean that they are a different sort of stuff or substance. They are not substantial in the sense that physical things are. They are immaterial. They can't exist by themselves or in isolation but they can be incorporated in vastly different bearers. The same logic can be expressed in very many different ways. Many languages use the same alphabet. The same geometrical relations are expressed in many different materials. Sign relations don't function only in brains but in books and scientific apparatus, in economic systems and religious rituals, and a host of other bearers, almost certainly in ways we can hardly imagine at present. Consciousness is only a colourful flower that depends on enormously complex underpinnings of which it gives hardly any indication, much less understanding.

Although mental relations may not have independent powers in the way physical agents do, they do have very distinctive structures and functions. The physical bearers of intentional relations can convey messages only in so far as they conform to the stringent laws governing the particular system of signifiers that they serve. Until the advent of computers in the sixties our main examples of this subservience were inactive, marks on paper and sounds. They had effects, of course, which enabled them to transmit messages, but they did not construct messages themselves in the way that computers do. Computers use signs interactively, not just correcting spelling and generating warnings but performing complex calculations, checking their own performance, adaptively controlling physical processes and so on. It is clear that the human brain is very much more complex than the sort of computers that we can construct on the knowledge we have at present. If we want to understand the role of the brain in supporting mental activity we need first to construct much better analyses of mental relations, their networking structures and their intentional dynamics, than we have at present. Only then will we be in a position to understand how they can be embodied in complex physical processes.

Against Dichotomy

Many philosophers had tried to get beyond the mind-matter dichotomy by various forms of monism, all pretty clearly unsuccessful, ranging from the doctrine that the material world is an illusion to the crudest mechanistic materialism. What they all had in common was the conviction that they could establish with finality, on purely general, a priori grounds, what the world was made of, and that grasping the implications of this truth was fundamental to the way we should live our lives. This is true only in its negative aspect. There is no point in invoking powers that do not exist or in treating the illusory as if it made a difference to what really happens. But, as the surprises of the course of organic evolution show, it is folly to imagine that we have any conception of the variety of possibilities that new forms of organisation can open up. It seemed clear to me that so far genetics had succeeded only in discovering the alphabet and a few of the simplest messages of the genomes of various organisms. The grammar through which indefinitely more complex messages might be constructed remains to be discovered.

We are too easily impressed by the raw power of basic physical forces. Form, spirit, significance and purpose operate in a different way, not by some distinctive kind of force, but by allowing only those conjunctions of elements that conform to their requirements to form stable and reproducible operating systems to survive, adapt, regulate and reproduce themselves. We can understand these things only if we are prepared to explore new ways of organisation, new concepts and possibilities. There is no such thing as an ultimate framework of understanding. The ways in which forms of sustainable activity proliferate continually generate surprises, as unpredictable advances in mathematics so clearly demonstrate.

General metaphysical schemes can be a matter of interesting speculative argument, but there can be no knock down arguments in such matters. As the history of logic and mathematics shows, progress in thinking at the highest levels of abstraction and generality is full of surprises. Materialism is always prone to treating the current state of scientific theory as if it supplied the ultimate set of categories that metaphysicians had sought. The physicist's search for a unitary basic theory must go on, but one must always remember that such a theory is a very poor indicator of what powers complexes of basic components may develop. A theory in physics, for example, is required to sustain the claim that it can explain the phenomena to which it applies completely, without residue. But that is very different from claiming that in some other respect what underlies these phenomena may not be theorised differently but equally appropriately in another set of relationships. There is no reason to think even the best of our concepts exhaust the reality to which they apply.

On the other hand, we do have good grounds for scepticism about gods and ghosts and supernatural agencies generally, and that scepticism is quite reasonably taken to have practical consequences. It is folly to rely on the intervention of some dubious spirit healer when empirically proven remedies are available. Indeed there is a general need to evaluate our ways of dealing with our problems in terms of sound knowledge of their effectiveness. We have to reject the sort of subjectivism that condemns as unwarranted any attempt to treat others as being mistaken in believing in practices that are in fact harmful to them. At the very least, where the effects of mistaken belief have serious consequences for others, those beliefs must be challenged. Finding the appropriate ways of doing this without undermining people's self-esteem and independence is often very difficult. We do have to persuade people that the effective barrier against AIDS is not a charm but a condom.

As the seventies moved on I became increasingly dissatisfied with analytical philosophy, still the ruling mode of philosophising in the Anglophone world. What philosophers and their customers traditionally looked for was a set of comprehensive concepts that interpreted the whole of reality in a way that illuminated all their important value choices by singling out those aspects of reality that are really real and consequently really valuable. Analytic philosophy had abandoned that ambition. Taking a 'linguistic turn' it concentrated for a time on the analysis of our ways of talking about things, rather than on what was talked about. It was concerned to analyse the language of science rather than its substantive findings or presuppositions. Metaethics, the study of normative utterances, pretended to be neutral about substantive moral questions. As an exclusive focus that proved very unsatisfactory, and attention soon expanded to encompass substantive questions, but with a very strong concentration on what could be established as a matter of objective truth. This also proved very constricting. Speculative thinking can be very important, provided its hazardous character is acknowledged.

In contemporary academic philosophy the tendency was to deny any strong connection between fact and value, thus undercutting any pretension to supply a guide to living. In so far as it was directed against traditional pretensions to base ethics on metaphysical doctrines about our nature and destiny or popular assumptions about the limits of 'human nature' it was salutary. But it neglected the exploration of the ways in which social structures and relationships were interconnected with human values. The theoretical ambitions of traditional philosophers were also suspect, because, in the attempt to cover everything of importance, they were driven to oversimplify, over-generalise and make dubious claims about the validity of arguments. As Wittgenstein said, philosophers feed on just one type of example.

The strength of analytic philosophy is that it is acutely aware of the dangers of generalising. It seeks to avoid them by testing philosophical assertions against counter examples. Unfortunately, the imagined counter examples are always thinly described, and all the testing amounts to is an appeal to our 'intuitions' about how we would describe such a case. For example, the accepted definition of knowledge is 'justified true belief'. So philosophers try to imagine cases where a person might have a true belief and be justified in holding that belief, but would not be described as knowing that the belief is true, in the ordinary sense of 'know'. Such puzzles do indeed have their uses, but they are very limited. The whole procedure puts an inordinate weight on conventional linguistic usage, which in turn may well be confused, or, as Keynes said of economic 'common sense', just repeating the opinions of some dead philosopher. Also, this way of testing generalisations often highlights fringe cases where some of a concept's central connections no longer hold and the point of the concept is lost. The analytic philosophers want philosophy to be a respectable academic discipline with sound, objectively accessible methods, analogous to those of science. But it can't be like that.

My view is that philosophy has to give up pretensions to providing a sort of universal guide to what we should prefer or in what terms we should think of things. But it need not become merely academic, of little practical relevance. Instead it should occupy itself with drawing attention to aspects of our situation that we are likely to ignore or misconceive and with trying to suggest new perspectives on old problems or new problems of which we are hardly aware. Such activity can result in major shifts of perspective such as traditional philosophy sought, without the dubious universalistic or reductionist tactics that so often characterised it. Old philosophy can still be of use, not just in providing reminders of how easily we can get things wrong or reminding us of problems that they were right to be concerned about even when they misconstrued them, but also in giving us a benchmark against which we can measure the specific novelty of the problems that now confront us in the light of what we now know and of the changes in our ways of living. Even 'eternal' problems change as what we can know and do changes. Philosophers should be seen mainly as making suggestions, 'assembling reminders for a purpose', as Wittgenstein put it.

To some unquantifiable degree all of us live our lives in a network of what from an externalised scientific perspective are mistaken beliefs, illusions and misunderstandings. Many of these are intersubjective, the result of the particular perspective on things that we share as human beings, with our limited sensory equipment and conceptual resources, in thrall to psychological needs that were developed in very different circumstances from our present ones. All our poetry and arts, our moralities and identities, sensibilities and spontaneous intuitions are built up on this intersubjective matrix. To reject it, to attempt to think of our lives exclusively in the categories of the sciences is not only impossible but radically impoverishing of everything that gives meaning to life. We cannot live by objective truth alone. Enriching our lives involves exploring and expanding the intersubjective world, finding new perceptions, new practices, new aspirations, incorporating as much as we can of the scientific understanding of the matrix of our lives into human uses. In this process old ways of thinking about, explaining and evaluating things change in ways that only in retrospect become fully apparent. In differing respects there is progress and loss, much of it necessarily unconcluded and only inconclusively assessable.

In the light of these considerations I became much more sympathetic to the views of those who wanted to involve philosophy strongly in the exploration of the intersubjective world rather than concentrating exclusively on the objectivised worlds of science and metaphysics.[1] So I was immediately receptive when feminists came forward to point out that human intersubjectivity was not as uniform as philosophers and others had assumed, but was structured socially and culturally on a base of biological and other differences between the sexes. Philosophy must not only recognise the suppressed problems that now emerged, but play its part in rectifying the harm

---

1 It should be clear that I think that a great deal of harm has been done by attempts to give a unitary view of human knowledge and of truth. Among contemporary postmodernists the tendency is to emphasise the conventional and historically conditioned character of all language and symbolisation. From that point of view it is easy to fall into seeing objectified entities as especially illusory, the result of failing to see that the concepts in which they are represented are artificial constructions. Such constructions may happen to work, to serve certain practical ends, but there can be no ground for thinking that we can explain why some constructions work while others do not. The temptation to think that they work because of some close correspondence between the structures of certain of our representations and the structures of the things to which they apply must be resisted. It is mere dogmatism.

This is a point that still needs to be made. But if this is taken as all that is to be said about the matter one is left in the relativist position that eschews all programmatic evaluation. On the contrary, there are grounds for evaluation, sometimes objective, sometimes intersubjective. There are facts, even when the precise form they take involves some arbitrary decisions. Draw an arbitrary line in the sand. It is an objective fact that some grains of sand are on one side of the line and others are not, although it is equally clear that the sort of division one makes by dragging a stick through the sand is imprecise and probably insignificant. But many procedures and the facts they isolate have connections that are not arbitrary. They connect not just in symbolisation but causally with other facts, enabling us to test certain forms of representation and have confidence in others in certain contexts, on objective, though rarely completely conclusive, grounds.

done to women under the practices that male power had entrenched. This mission was not just academic, but social and political.

The Sixties Revolution

Calling the mission of philosophy social and political was a symptom of the times. Political motivations had always been important in the issues on which philosophers concentrated and in the considerations to which they gave importance. Most philosophers since the eighteenth century had sought to undermine the doctrinal foundations of authoritarianism in order to weaken the social underpinnings of authoritarian religions and regimes. The point of using philosophy for such purposes is destroyed if the process of philosophical debate is reduced to political tactics. So philosophers have usually been anxious to keep political considerations at arms length. That is easily done where they are confident that they will triumph in the long run, but where there is a forceful demand for immediate and radical change political considerations come to the fore. That was the situation in the late sixties and early seventies.

The postmodernist prejudice against objectivity is an extreme offshoot of the rationalist project of freeing humanity from illusions. In reaction against foundationalism, it refuses to consider the variety of contexts in which we speak of truth and justification. The remedy is to pay attention to the enormous range of ways in which instances of different kinds of representation may be criticised as deficient in relation to others of their kind or praised as being more significant in certain ways than some other instance. Only where the issue reduces to a narrow alternative of which the other prong is demonstrable falsity is truth the relevant characterisation of a representation. The markings on a map need to correspond to identifiable objects on the surface of the earth and exhibit certain relations between them. Maps might seem prime candidates for truth. But we call good maps 'accurate' rather than 'true', because accuracy is a matter of degrees and is always relative to practical needs. We are tempted to appeal to truth when we should be thinking in other terms, because it so readily conveys the aura of authoritative decision, especially in practical matters of great importance. Truth in such matters is rarely available, but there are very many other considerations, both objective and intersubjective, that can be relevant and even decisive for practical purposes.

Liberation from all forms of oppression was the order of the day. Traditional philosophy had sought wisdom and wisdom consisted in understanding and conforming to the basic course of nature in which society was embedded. Now the postwar generation rallied to the slogan of Marx's eleventh thesis on Feuerbach: 'Until now philosophers have been content to understand the world. The task is to change it'. A popular parody added: 'Until now the world has been content to understand philosophers. The task is to change them'. Radical dissent from tradition was nothing new, but previously it had generally had an individualistic orientation, pitting the free individual or an enlightened coterie against an oppressive society. At most it cherished the hope that ultimately the example of the enlightened might bring about a general social change. The new movement wanted immediate social, political and cultural change for the whole world. It chanted insistently: 'What do we want? Liberation. When do we want it? NOW!'

It is difficult to convey how vividly and confidently this change expressed itself in every aspect of the attitudes and behaviour, not just of university students, but of young people more generally. Rock concerts, fuelled by pot and speed, became the religious rites through which the new sensibility was amplified with overwhelming power. Clothing, hair, body language, graffiti and iconography of every kind created an overwhelmingly new environment. The young felt that they had taken over everyday life and that nobody could stop them dismantling the Bastilles of traditional power. Radicals and liberals of the older generations mostly looked on with a mixture of wonder, sympathy and disquiet. Only a few, concerned that the movement to 'Make Love, Not War' undermined the resistance of Western nations to the spread of totalitarian communism, put up any concerted resistance. Faced with the call to take a stand I had no doubt that I would line up with those who said 'Better Red than Dead', even if that did mean weakening opposition to Red imperialism. I did not believe that such imperialism could succeed in the long run.

Orwell's *Nineteen Eighty-Four* could not last, but thermonuclear war might do irreversible damage. The dream of liberation could never be effectively suppressed. The hollow pretences of Big Brother would always be undercut by the violent means required to prop them up.

At the same time the Vietnam War and the global political strategies that surrounded it continued to put an unbearable strain on the claims of the West to be the Free World. Repressive regimes were consistently supported and democratic regimes that seemed at all unreliable subverted in the all-consuming fight against communism. The commercial interests of multinational corporations were the most obvious beneficiaries of the economic and political policies that the so-called Cold War imposed on nations throughout the world. It was not surprising that reactions to this situation took increasingly anarchist forms, rejecting as illegitimate not just the explicit policies of the military-industrial complex, but the legitimacy of political authority in all its existing forms. Ultimately I agreed with the anarchists that the state is beyond redemption, the problem, not the answer. Monopolising supreme power is intrinsically flawed. But I rejected their implicit faith in the capacity of spontaneous self-organising communities to supplant the state as the basic organ of collective decision-making. The problem was too complex for either a comprehensive plan or no plan at all. Solving it was a matter of finding and gradually entrenching new, decentred but formalised and authoritative ways of dealing with the complex and difficult problems of modern societies.

In some respects the turmoil of those few years in the late sixties and early seventies marked decisive and lasting changes. Sexual relations of all sorts between consenting adults were no longer thought of in connection with the institutions of marriage and family. They became just a question of the desires and sensibilities of individuals. Dress, language and comportment, by becoming a matter of comfort, ease and personal preferences, tore down much of the fabric of traditional social signifiers. Prestigious institutions gave up their claims to authority, no longer telling people what was right or wise, but attempting to respond to the demands of their clients. These changes survived the demise of radicalism because they were coopted and consolidated by consumer-oriented capitalism, encouraging and catering to every demand that could be exploited commercially. With the aid of new communications technologies the counterculture was industrialised and entrenched. Ways of thinking changed as well, and many young philosophers strove to articulate a new kind of understanding and a new set of topics.

In other respects the revolution failed to achieve any decisive movement in the directions towards which it was supposed to be directed, especially participatory democracy and richer, fuller community life. The individualist, consumerist pattern triumphed and spawned the managerial revolution in which effectiveness and efficiency were equated with the power of managers to monopolise decision-making and implementation, constrained only by the requirements of short-term market success. Broadly based participation in constructive decision-making was no longer regarded as in any way desirable. From the systemic point of view it could only be costly, slow and inexpert. From the point of view of the individual it was an unnecessary waste of time and an encouragement to intrusive busybodies. The only participation the consumer needed was at the point of sale or, in political matters, at the ballot box. The mobility of modern living destroyed the ties of local identity and fixed roles. The only communities that mattered were those a person chose to join and could leave at will.

I was deeply torn by these developments. As a reformed defender and abettor of the authoritarianism of the church, I felt bound to make amends by endorsing the anti-authoritarianism of the young. The counterculture was not to my taste, but I strove to understand it, distrustful of the matrix in which my own tastes had been formed. I admired the determination and dedication of many of the activists, but I feared the simplistic ideas on which they so often based their actions and the intoxicating rhetoric of liberation. I was a committed democrat, but acutely conscious of the authoritarian dangers of hypostasising 'the people'. I was also disturbed by the tendency to lapse into consumerism and managerialism.

What I looked for in democracy was a process in which people explored freely and responsibly their various collective interests and opportunities. I looked for ways in which people learned in practice to appreciate and facilitate each other's interests, setting up ways of making good decisions and implementing them flexibly and humanely. The characteristic practices of the new radicals did not produce these results. Decisions were made at open meetings with no fixed rules about who could take part or what decisions were valid. At mass meetings, harangued by forceful speakers, vague resolutions were endorsed by acclamation. Most of those present had no idea of the implications of what they were proclaiming as their will. At the other extreme, small committees with tenuous claims to be representative of their purported constituencies committed their followers to dubious policies and tactics on the authority of their role as leaders. As long as it was just a question of putting pressure on established authorities to respond to popular demands on an ad hoc basis, such proceedings could be justified, but in the context of genuine differences of interests and opinions they were dangerous and destructive of sound decisions. They could not make, much less implement, constructive decisions. The problem of effective democracy forced itself on my attention as I struggled to deal with the politicisation of our department.

Politics in Academia

The philosophy department could hardly remain untouched by the emergence of the new student radicalism. Looking for an account of what was wrong with their society, many radicals found it in Marx's analysis of capitalism. Many of the younger generation were attracted most strongly to the earlier, more humanist Marx with his theme of alienation and how to transcend it. Some, however, were drawn to a more scientific reading of Marx's work focused on *Capital*. Among these were two members of the department, Wal Suchting, well established in the profession as a very competent philosopher of science, and Michael Devitt, recently back from Harvard, full of enthusiasm for a causal theory of meaning. They were determined to add courses on Marxism to the department curriculum and went about doing so in a very provocative manner.

The department was already deeply divided. David Armstrong and David Stove, growing away from the libertarian sympathies of their youth, became increasingly alarmed at the way in which radical students were undermining authority of all sorts and especially at the ways in which they weakened the West, which they saw as in danger from the drive of communism towards world domination. Armstrong saw it as his right as a professor and his duty as a citizen to fight against the radicals in the university. This had already led to a number of battles over appointments and over democratisation of decision-making in which he had been opposed by a majority of department staff, including me. When Suchting and Devitt put forward their proposal for courses on Marxism-Leninism, including works by Mao, with a clear political purpose, he strove to have them disallowed. The courses were finally approved in a somewhat less provocative guise as Marxism I and II.

In 1973 Margaret and I took study leave for six months near Oxford. Returning to Sydney we found the majority of staff and students in philosophy, together with some others in the faculty, on strike over the issue of a proposed course in feminism. One of the key objections to the proposal was that responsibility for giving and assessing the course was to be given to two tutors who had not been appointed as lecturers, Jean Curthoys and Liz Jacka. Finally the course was allowed on the understanding that I would be in charge of the work, with the assistance of the original proponents. This was too much for Armstrong and five other senior members of the department. They petitioned the Vice-Chancellor to institute a separate department for them, to be called Traditional and Modern Philosophy (T&M). Otherwise, they would be forced to resign in the face of an intolerable situation. The Vice-Chancellor, Bruce Williams, summoned me and asked whether, if he were to grant this request, I would undertake the headship of the rump department. The rump were strongly disposed to resist the separation and several of them sought positions elsewhere. However, the separation was accepted, rejecting the suggestion of 'Critical and Contemporary Philosophy' in favour of the meaningless 'General Philosophy' (GP).

The radical image of GP attracted great numbers of students and insoluble problems. It inherited from the last days of the old department an agreement that in matters of department decision every member, staff or student, should have an equal vote. The result was chronic instability, especially as attendance at meetings fluctuated wildly. At regular weekly meetings attended by staff and mainly senior students with a strong commitment to the continuance of GP, discussion was rational and well-informed. But when issues became divisive, mass meetings of hundreds of students were polarised by inflammatory speeches and politicised resolutions were passed. The staff, most of whom had little reason for being in the department other than opposition to what they saw as Armstrong's authoritarianism, began to split into factions. A number sought entry into T&M, where peace and harmony prevailed, while others sought appointments elsewhere. The burden on the remaining staff was enormous.

Marxism and Feminism

Finally, recognising that the problem of student numbers was not going to go away, the Vice-Chancellor agreed that four lectureships in the department should be advertised, and after much negotiation appointments were made. The most important were those of Gyorgy Markus, a distinguished Hungarian from the school of Lukacs, an unorthodox Marxist, and Paul Crittenden, a Catholic priest with an Oxford background and Sydney associations. They were both to become professors and very influential throughout the Faculty of Arts, which twice elected Paul as Dean. Jean Curthoys was finally made a lecturer and Lloyd Reinhardt, a genial American with wide interests, joined the department. In addition, following a reorganisation in the Faculty of Science, Alan Chalmers, a well-known philosopher of science joined the staff of GP. While they solved some of the difficulties of the department, other conflicts continued to threaten it. In particular new antagonisms arose over Marxism and feminism.

The leader of the Marxists was Wal Suchting, with whom I became closely associated, in spite of fundamental differences of temperament, background, political ideology and practical assessments of our situation and its problems. Wal's instincts and theoretical convictions led him to emphasise conflict and see progress as emerging from confrontation of opposing positions in both theoretical and political contexts. He was a Leninist in the Trotskyite tradition, bookish, immersed, like Trotsky, in an extraordinarily wide scientific, literary and musical culture. He was contemptuous of conventional morality, embracing an ethos of dedication to the revolution in which pretty well anything could be justified if it could be shown to advance the cause. He found my tendency to go to almost any length to downplay conflicts and construct compromises 'idealist' and so theoretically and politically wrong. Naturally Wal's overt political convictions and their occasional implementation in department decision-making led to confrontations that I strove unsuccessfully to contain and to successive defections of staff from the department, amid accusations of manipulation and political intolerance.

In company with a small but very sophisticated network in the UK and USA Suchting and others found a new and very congenial counter to the wishy-washy humanist Marxism of popular radicalism in the work of the French philosopher, Louis Althusser. Building on the work of the French tradition in philosophy of science, best known through the writings of Gaston Bachelard, Althusser emphasised that getting anywhere with the task of understanding any important aspect of reality depended on having the right concepts and procedures of analysis. Without the right conceptual tools there could be no genuine understanding, and those tools were produced in historic revolutions that opened up new continents of theory. In physics Newton, in biology Darwin, in psychology Freud and in social theory Marx, each broke away from the mess that preceded them to give clear shape to a science that was henceforth in a position to develop securely and fruitfully from that starting point. In the case of Marx that set of tools was produced in breaking away from the early humanist meanderings to the firm theoretical framework of *Capital*.

While I was very sympathetic to the thesis of the importance of the right concepts to fruitful understanding, I was unconvinced by the scientific pretensions of both Marxism and Freudianism, although recognising the importance of much of what they drew attention to. A scientific theory, as the Althusserians emphasised, gives an explanation of the phenomena it identifies that is complete and precise. The point of claiming scientific status for Marxism, properly understood, was to exclude its competitors from serious consideration. Of course, there would be differences within Marxism and probably revolutionary developments analogous to those of relativity and quantum mechanics, but these must arise from grappling with problems within the enterprise, using the tools that were characteristic of it. The sciences, on this view, did not just observe reality. They interacted with it. The basic form of Marxist interaction with reality was the class struggle. Theory developed in and through the class struggle.

This extremely dubious analogy between the process of experimentation in the physical sciences and the class struggle seemed both conceptually obscure and gratuitous. It appealed only because it served the political purpose of discrediting the views of those who failed to engage wholeheartedly in the struggle. It sounded uncomfortably like the Stalinist prostitution of science to authoritarian political tactics. Althusser attempted to escape this condemnation by introducing his theory of ideology as the means of understanding the nature of class struggle in the realm of theory not as political tactics, but as an indispensable part of the scientific enterprise. As against the tendency of vulgar Marxism to portray ideology as lies promoted by the ruling class to fool the proletariat, Althusser depicted ideology as a pervasive and unavoidable aspect of human thinking. We live our ordinary lives in a world of experiences constituted by things that have no place in a scientific view of the world.

Empiricism, in the broad sense in which Althusser uses the term, consists in taking the tropes of everyday experience as the matrix of our understanding what is really going on. Just as in physics we have to get away from such superficial concepts as hardness, or in biology see adaptation by natural selection instead of a maker's design, so in social matters we have to get away from such concepts as greed or conspiracy to grasp the structural nature of the socio-economic system and what needs to happen for a new system to emerge. There will always be ideology. We will always live immersed in it. Only in very special contexts can we break through its grip. In the physical sciences we must join the scientific community grappling with physical reality. In the social sciences we must join the community of those who are grappling with the real forces that determine the course of history. Only that community will not be put off with superficial, comfortably self-serving accounts of what affects them. Only in their struggle to remake the world will they develop real understanding of it.

In my view Althusser had a point in emphasising the need to break away from mere empiricism and the importance of scientific communities as the contexts in which it is possible to do so in specific areas of enquiry. But I could not accept either the view that our life-world was merely an obfuscation or the subjugation of all other human interests and aspirations to the allegedly scientific framework of class struggle. After all, the motivation for class struggle had to be ideological in Althusser's terms. Marxism in the Althusserian framework was just one more instance of the invocation of privileged access to the truth as the warrant for authority. It had no clear content beyond a highly simplistic and dogmatic economic theory in which economic roles were explained in terms of crude dichotomies. Relations of production were given a hypostasised reality that had only the remotest relations with the complexities of the actual development of social and political history.

Feminists resisted the reduction of their struggle to a minor aspect of class struggle, of no independent theoretical significance. They also rejected scientistic models of understanding. Students interested in the role ways of thinking and feeling played in constituting social formations turned increasingly to such writers as Foucault, with his rapidly changing ideas about forms of power, social practices and ways of representing them. Others followed up various lines of investigation coming from reinterpretations of Freud, linking with theories of the imaginary, of signifiers, of bodies and embodiment. The proliferation of diverse approaches, especially in Paris, generated a movement that soon came to be called postmodernism. Not only did it shrug off the scientific pretensions of Marxism and classical social theory generally. Increasingly it undertook to pull science down from its honoured pedestal, with mixed results.

The Althusserians were routed. When Althusser himself, having murdered his wife, was declared insane, it seemed a judgement on his whole enterprise. Suchting retreated into strictly scholarly pursuits, lamenting the degeneration of serious engagement with history into trivialities and intellectual anarchy. There was, indeed, a lot of verbiage being thrown around that disguised its vacuity under provocatively sexy fashions. But there was also a great deal of enduring importance that emerged from the confusion, especially in the work of such people as Moira Gatens and Paul Patten, both of whom later returned from appointments elsewhere to chairs in Sydney, Paul Redding, also later a professor in Sydney, and Liz Grosz, who had a distinguished career in the US, to mention only a few. My role was confined to making space in which such people could work and taking an interest in what they were doing, without making much contribution to it.

Ethics

In common with other senior staff, I continued to provide courses on more traditional lines. I attached particular importance to ethics. Current Anglophone theories were split into three camps. The utilitarians, or, as they tended to prefer, consequentialists, held that the rightness of an action should be judged only by its consequences for human happiness. What maximised the happiness of mankind as a whole, or of all sentient beings, was right. This view was full of difficulties. It seemed to hold that the good of a particular individual should always be sacrificed whenever it stood in the way of the preferences of a greater number of others. It seems irresponsible not to take the consequences of an action into account in assessing its moral worth, but that is not the only moral consideration. The end does sometimes justify the means, but not always.

A second view, called in the jargon deontologist, insisted that morality was a matter of strictly universal rules and that one should act in such a way that if everybody in the same situation acted in the same way the outcome would be perfectly compatible with the freedom and dignity of all concerned. One may not tell lies, since if everybody told lies whenever it suited them, communication and trust between human beings would collapse. This view easily degenerates into a negative and over-rigid conception. Surely there are occasions when a lie may be justified to avert some great evil.

Rules are important, especially in protecting the basic rights of persons, but conformity to rules is not what morality is about, and justifying rules is a complex process.

The third main contender as a theory of morality was that the point of morality is virtue, the cultivation of those dispositions that befit human beings in their relations with each other. This has the merit of a positive focus that puts rules and calculations of consequences in a motivational context. However, apart from being rather vague and inadequate as a criterion of what is right, especially in matters of justice, emphasis on the cultivation of virtue suggests a sort of athleticism of virtue focused on building up one's moral muscle. Even though self-approval is fundamentally important, it needs to be negotiated socially.

The point that I strove to make is that it is a radical mistake to look for a theory of any of these kinds as giving an exclusive account of right action, much less of what is morally admirable. Considerations of all three kinds, and of other sorts as well, are relevant in very many contexts. There is no way of determining in general how each is to be balanced against the others. Even when in a particular context it is clear that certain considerations are more relevant than others to that context, the relative weight to be attached, say, to conflicting rights may be very much a matter of opinion. What is important is not to exclude relevant considerations or to reduce one kind of consideration to another at the cost of abstracting from much that constitutes its particular relevance to certain kinds of situation. Thus the utilitarian will protest that, of course, rules are important so that we can know where we stand with each other, and they can't be passed over lightly. And virtue is important, obviously, if we are to perform reliably. But the central question about virtue is not its usefulness as a good habit, but what we see as befitting a human being. Similarly, rules are especially important where basic human rights are at issue, embodying our conception of human beings as never reducible to means to some collective end. Not all rules are just rules of thumb, to be judged by their utility.

Ethics, in this perspective, was another instance of the wisdom of Wittgenstein's warnings against looking for theories in the scientific sense in philosophical matters. The task of philosophy is not to reduce the range of considerations in any matter to some simple decision procedure, but to fight against our tendencies to oversimplification. In this respect, it is the contrary of what has most often been seen as the point of philosophy, namely to have a clear and universally applicable set of priorities based on a well-grounded view of the point of it all. A person may properly develop such a point of view in constructing his or her own life, but we quite rightly emphasise that others will look at things differently. There is no ultimate all-embracing truth in such an enterprise. That is not to say that anything goes. There are many specific truths about our biology and psychology, as well about the concepts available to us, that we ignore at our peril.

It is also important in many contexts to fight against the intrusion of irrelevancies into questions that are otherwise clear, as, for example when we reject the fact that slavery is traditional in some societies as a justification for continuing it. But, equally, we need to be wary of too peremptory ways of dismissing some considerations as irrelevant. There is no substitute for serious discussion aimed at giving every aspect of a question due weight by exploring its interconnections, proceeding by analogy, envisaging different cases and precedents. Morality needs to be seen not just as some set of constraints imposed on human conduct, but also as an enriching aspect of human action, a matter of the significant relations that together we create and validate in the process of trying to find satisfying and sustaining ways of living together.

This constructive view of morality is not the whole story. There are both personal and social evils, murder, rape and dehumanisation on the one hand, and slavery, aggressive war and radical deprivation on the other, which are not to be treated as unfortunate side-effects of the quest for higher ends. The things we call evils are not like undesirable aspects of a proposal that we weigh against its benefits. We must not only abstain from doing evil things but strive to prevent them and, where possible rectify them. Those who fail to recognise this place themselves outside the bounds of moral dialogue. Evils can be tolerated only hesitantly, reluctantly and in extreme cases, by the imperative necessity of avoiding greater evils. Any dialogue in such matters almost inevitably excludes the participation of those on whom evils are inflicted. At best sympathetic or fearful proxies may object to justifications of evil in the particular case. There is a great deal to be said for the position that, especially in the treatment of those who are a burden on us, we should hedge ourselves in with absolute moral prohibitions, recognising that our judgement in such cases is not to be trusted.

Because our morality is bound up with the institutions, practices and sensitivities of the communities in which we live, and these are always open to revision, occasions may arise when we feel bound to step beyond the moral consensus, taking on ourselves a deserved moral condemnation, doing something for which there are no accepted excuses. We cannot ignore the judgement of our peers, but in the long run we must each justify our selves before the impartial observer that we construct from critical reflection on our own experience. There is no guarantee that all moral problems are solvable.

Such questions are extremely disputable, because the nature and scope of morality is not something given a priori, *pace* Kant. It is a construction that we have to work on continually in the light of changing sensibilities, possibilities and social relationships. It does not allow us, individually or collectively, to mount the vacant throne of God, to prescribe for others without their having a say about what we consider justifiable. Again, moral values are not the only ones. Aesthetic, scientific, economic and many other activities have their own values and purposes, independently of the moral virtues, even where moral virtues such as integrity and fairness are relevant to them. In the pursuit of such ends morality is a matter of side-constraints or boundaries. Moral considerations are quite inadequate to direct what needs to be done to further them. Moralism, reducing all values to moral values, is destructive of human welfare. When morality is concerned about advancing welfare, it needs to take non-moral values into account as independently life-enhancing.

Morality, Democracy and Life

Morality must be based on personal and communal experience. A living, binding morality cannot be generated by academic or detached discussions. They can only clarify it. Much less can it be handed down by authority. It must arise out of a process of discussion and acceptance of each other by participants in the relevant roles and relationships. Above all, it must be sustained by social practices in which moral dialogue and negotiation are enacted and institutionalised. Today the family is in many ways a powerful forum of moral discussion of the problems in living together in close relationships. Where it now rests on continuing mutual consent of partners rather than legal status and on the education of children in genuinely constructive rather than authoritarian and punitive practices, moral dialogue is inherent in family life. The surprising, if still limited, success of the movement to improve the status and roles of women owes much to the way in which it has become understood and accepted in the family context. Similarly, in many other kinds of associations and institutions, forms of decision-making and of interaction have vastly improved. The terms of membership and participation have given much greater weight to the individual needs and desires, encouraging discussion, embracing diversity rather than uniformity and flexibility rather than rigidity.

It has always seemed to me that construing morality as law, even divine law, is inherently self-defeating to the extent that law depends on sanctions to ensure obedience. The conviction that all human beings are incorrigible sinners relies on a model that assumes that they will not do the right thing except from fear of sanctions and that sanctions are inevitably in a dim and distant future while temptation is in the vivid and immediate present. Granted that the urgent desires of people are often in conflict with the desires of others and even with their own longer term and more important interests, law takes the form of a restraint that must overpower desire, a negation of satisfaction rather than a promise of more enduring happiness. Only where self-discipline in pursuit of satisfying achievements, virtue, is seen as rewarding and attainable can we hope to get beyond the law, as St Paul vainly promised the early Christians. That can only happen when people can not only direct their private lives to worthwhile ends, but can also, if they wish, participate effectively in shaping those public decisions that most strongly affect them. Virtue is a matter of power. It flourishes when people have effective responsibility for their choices and a sensitive understanding of what they involve.

Again, what matters most to us is the opinion of our peers. To the extent that the law is alien, contrary to our desires, we often have a common interest with our closest peers in encouraging each other to ignore or defy it, establishing our own norms to suit ourselves. As long as the subcultures in which such norms are generated and applied are divorced from or even alienated from any context of fulfilment through the exercise of wider social roles, the claims of wider morality will suffer in competition with the norms of the subculture. At best publicly endorsed standards will appear as the demands of respectability, requiring only external and often hypocritical conformity. That in turn converges with a robust scepticism about the motives of those who appear to be concerned about moral probity. The consequence is corruption of public life. Politicians, being no longer trusted, give up the struggle to be trustworthy. The making of public morality cannot be delegated to professionals. Effective freedom of participation in responsible decision-making is essential to a realistic, effective and constructive public morality. Mere idealism breeds cynicism.

Human Fulfilment and Dialogue

The position at which I had arrived was that morality in its broadest sense is enormously complex in ways best illustrated by analogy with the arts. Much of it consists of performances, ways in which we re-enact standard scripts, undertaking obligations, pledging loyalties, expressing recognition, that have a host of significant connections in virtue of the established force of the signifiers and practices of which they are instances. Like it or not, by our performances we undertake obligations and render ourselves subject to moral appraisal. From some points of view the ineluctable pressures on us to perform in approved fashion in order to achieve most of our desires is a sort of slavery, binding us to the endless repetition of actions that benefit others or 'society' at the expense of our capacity to satisfy our own impulses. At the personal level we may feel like shop assistants forced to smile at customers we would love to insult. At the political level we may feel completely alienated from and oppressed by the whole structure of our social context.

Change the perspective, and everything is transformed. Our capacity to undertake obligations, pledge loyalties and express relationships is what makes possible an open-ended process of enriching our lives by creating meaningful, intersubjective connections in which we can find infinitely varied fulfilment. Especially where we succeed in enlivening our performances with a distinctive personal emotional quality, we invite not just routine responses but an equally personal recognition from others that confirms our values, our satisfaction with ourselves and our sense of community. As in artistic performances, there is a tension between the inevitable drift into banality through repetition and the necessity for firmly established signifiers as the basis of all communication.

That tension can be resolved only by a constant effort on the part of key performers to reinterpret the established tropes as new possibilities emerge and old connections become redundant.

In morality, as in the arts, that is necessarily a decentred, unorganised process, driven by the sensibilities of exceptional individuals who succeed in evoking a concerted response from a broad spectrum of people. New meanings become entrenched in ordinary discourse and in prevailing forms of evaluation. To the extent that everyday practice succeeds in living up to these standards, the change is inspiring and constructive. Often, however, it is not. Where we set ourselves impossible goals we invite despair about humankind and mutual denigration. I came to accept the view that the religious focus on fulfilment by escape from this corrupt world resulted from the failure of many religious cultures to generate an effective public morality.

The starting point of any public morality must be a comprehensive tolerance. The objective must be to allow as much scope as possible to all the desires with which different people find themselves encumbered by nature and nurture. Many of those desires will be ones that we wish others did not have. Some may be desires that we wish we ourselves did not have. Desires of all sorts proliferate incompatibilities. Dealing with them in practice is a matter of rejecting the temptation to rigidify them, in the name of some essentialist doctrine of human nature or some putative social necessity. Desires are mutable and incompatibilities are often a matter of scale and context. Preferences are rarely absolute and hardly ever cover all the relevant possibilities. Very often we can be in a position to make a practical choice only when we know what others will do. The rule, dear to bureaucrats, the envious and certain moralists, that if it is not possible for everybody to act in a certain way nobody should be allowed to do so, is absurd. Desires need to be negotiated, developed, facilitated or constrained according to the possibilities of fulfilling them without disproportionate inconvenience to the other desires of ourselves and other people. What is possible and what is best differ according to the particular circumstances in which we are placed. A great deal of this process of negotiation takes place in the ordinary course of informal life, but in large-scale societies many aspects of it need to be institutionalised. So many of our interactions are with strangers and so many of our desires are achievable only by organised action.

At the same time it is crucial to go beyond this individualist perspective. The point of communal decision-making has always been not merely to facilitate the pursuit of those ends that individuals can set themselves but to empower them to participate in enterprises that transcend their individual capacities and objectives, not just in scale but in kind. Such enterprises range from material achievements such as the great temples of older civilisations, with their supernatural significance, to the state considered as something of a higher kind of importance than the lives of its citizens. It has often been thought that identification with these higher enterprises confers worth on otherwise worthless human beings, who must be forced, if necessary, to sustain them. In rejecting such claims we need to recognise that there are many scientific, artistic, humanitarian and other creative enterprises of the highest importance that can only be pursued effectively if they are directed by authorities that have the power to make binding decisions, especially to mobilise and allocate resources.

In the recent past it has usually fallen to the state to perform these tasks, because of its monopoly of taxation, legislation and legal enforcement. We tend to see all such public goods from the perspective of nationalist conceptions of culture and of almost all forms of collective achievement. In a world in which both high and popular culture, science, technology and humanitarian concerns have taken on a global scope this chauvinism is increasingly absurd. Cultural protectionism is almost always stultifying. At the same time many people concerned about particular public goods are in revolt against the ways in which political and bureaucratic processes tend to impose inflexible solutions on diverse problems, stifling initiative and responsiveness to the needs of particular communities.

I came to be convinced that in thinking about political matters we should look for procedures that are most likely to produce decisions that are in the best interests of those most affected by them. This suggests a deliberative process involving people who are representative of the spectrum of those affected, seeking out creative solutions rather than voting on preset packages. They should be statistically representative of the people affected, not professional politicians chosen as representatives of political parties. The basic idea was that each distinct good should be subject to its own independent authority and that coordination among them should be by negotiation and arbitration rather than direction from any central authority. Of course, looked at in narrowly economic terms, such decision-processes would be expensive in terms of labour time, unless we count the opportunity to participate in the process as a benefit rather than a cost to the individuals concerned and the improved quality of collective decisions as a bonus to us all.

From Power Trading to Rational Decision

Decisions about the controlled production of public goods in the context of the nation state are a matter of concentrating power. In any complex polity the power of each political agent is a matter of their having the capacity to influence a wide range of decisions and to trade favours with other agents to increase their power. Typically one offers support that another values highly on an issue of little concern to oneself in return for support on some other issue about which one is more concerned. In everyday usage, to say that a decision was 'political' is to claim that it was determined by the power strategies of the politicians involved rather than the interests of those directly affected by the decision. It is to be expected that this process will often produce decisions that are sub-optimal as

means to their ostensible ends and a great deal of misrepresentation of what is happening. These poor results are often blamed on
the failings of politicians. In reality, if they are to get anything done,
politicians must win power in a system where almost everything is
traded against everything else, and no issue is decided on its own
merits alone.

The system persists because people love power. They cherish the
illusion that they can control a centralised government sufficiently
to ensure that the overall result is to empower them to control the
main features of their social life in their nation state and repulse what
seems to threaten them. This illusion is reinforced by the cult of the
leader, the chief executive to whom all good results are attributed,
fostering a false sense of security based on his power. Democratic
polities have sought to minimise the worst manifestations of this
illusion by constitutional restraints on power. Insisting on disclosure
of relevant information and holding the executive to account at the
next election ensures that power is accountable, at least in a very
general way. Nevertheless the extent and objects of that accountability
depend on the countervailing powers that can be mobilised against
the ruling coalition. Clearly how effective such provisions are is a
matter of the political assets and skills of the various players, the ways
in which constitutional rules and voting procedures allocate power,
and the extent to which money, advertising and misrepresentation
manipulate perceptions. We live in a world where 'wheeling and
dealing' determines the outcome of most issues and the ability to
'strike a deal' is much admired because it 'gets things done.' So hardly
anybody pays attention to the possibility that different decision
procedures might produce better decisions.

In many matters which choice is made out of a range of more or
less acceptable alternatives may not matter as much as that some clear
decision be taken and implemented. Nevertheless the overall social
consequences of power-driven decision-making are very destructive.
The interests of politically disadvantaged groups are ignored or

addressed only in terms of the ways in which they impact on the interests of the powerful. Even when such moral considerations as equality of opportunity are acknowledged, the opportunities that are seen as relevant are those of competing for wealth and power in the dominant pattern, not those of constructing diverse lifestyles. In such a context paternalism rules, at times harshly, punishing the hopeless for their predicament, but sometimes indulgently, encouraging irresponsibility. The only way such situations can be improved is by making those affected fully responsible for the decisions that control their opportunities. Both the paternalism of the welfare state and the plutocracy of the market must be rejected when it comes to essential public services.

The condition of such groups as black minorities in white nation states is an extreme instance of the perversion of public life that is almost universal. For over a century radical conservatives have argued that the *Welfare State is The Servile State* (Belloc, 1912) or *The Road to Serfdom* (Hayek, 1945). They made an important point. In the extreme cases of the Communist and Fascist one-party regimes the ubiquitous party machines ensured that everybody who professed subservience to them was provided with the necessities of life and rewarded for positive support. This routine subservience seems to have been a much more significant factor in maintaining those regimes than the punishments imposed on dissidents. People were corrupted and emasculated. At the same time they were often given the illusion of empowerment by being induced to identify with the more spectacular achievements of the regime.

In the Western democracies a more subtle form of corruption and subjection has emerged. In mass voting the electorate makes a choice about which of the packages offered by the major parties is the more attractive or offers better value for money. The promises on offer are often significantly unrealistic and voters are regularly disappointed. In part it is their own fault. They demand to be deceived, in politics as in many other matters, in societies where 'believing in something', especially oneself, is regarded as much more important than critical scrutiny of beliefs, and power-trading is regarded as an acceptable way of deciding what is to be done. People buy the packages on offer in much the same way as they buy a car. There is no way for them to know much about automotive engineering. They assume the professionals have done the best they can. They buy on price, image and conventional expectations, largely ignorant of and indifferent to the reasons why the packages on offer are constructed in the ways they are out of the alternatives that might be chosen. By and large, like car buyers, they guard against unpleasant surprises by sticking to the familiar, with concessions to fashionable presentation. Public goods are reduced to consumerist criteria. There is no room for active involvement of the customers in shaping the alternatives available.

It is completely unrealistic and perverse to insist that most voters should be very much better informed or invited to vote more frequently or on a much more detailed set of questions. It is impossible for anybody to be well informed about every significant issue. In practice all people can do is to protest loudly at the effects of bad decisions, usually too late to reverse them. How can we trust others to make decisions on our behalf? They must share our interests and bear the consequences of their decisions just as we do. My suggestion was that in the case of a large range of public goods where there are significant differences of interest the decisions should be in the hands of a committee that is statistically representative of the various legitmate interests most directly affected by those decisions. My hope was that in such circumstances the practice of genuine negotiation would become entrenched as the appropriate way of deciding the shape of public goods. Negotiation is apt to produce win-win outcomes to conflicting desires as each party attempts to offer to the other as much as possible at the least cost to itself. In serious negotiations one has to take the other's desires seriously. That in turn should produce a richer and more varied array of public goods than our present procedures. We need to give up the traditional democratic idea that government ought reflect the will of the people. What passes as the will of the people is a mythical distillation of largely unsound opinions. What matters is that it gives due consideration to the diversity of their interests. What those interests are is disclosed only by careful exploration of their situation by people who will bear the consequences of their decisions.

Such bodies eliminate generalised power trading. Their scope is limited to the specific issues with which they are entrusted. The negotiators can offer each other only concessions the cost of which falls on them. They will have to bear the direct consequences of their decisions. There is no point in trying to put an illusory 'spin' on what they are doing. It is to be expected that in the case of most such public goods a great many of the differences will involve moral considerations, such as the moral importance of different aspirations, traditional entitlements, genuine equality and so on. In taking such considerations seriously and exploring them responsibly I would hope that a more constructive and substantial moral climate would be generated and entrenched in the public culture, to the great benefit of all who participate in it. I hoped that a polity developed in this direction would produce a moral renovation vastly superior to what both individualistic liberalism and totalitarian ideologies had hoped to bring about. It would be both richer and more realistic. What we become and what we can desire is to a significant extent a matter of the things we can do together, and that in turn depends on the procedures and practices on which we can rely to enrich the context in which we live.

My prescription may look like an attempt to reduce the significance of moral inquiry to the impersonal decision theory. I prefer to think of it as a crucial part of an effective answer to the questions I set myself in my youth. Originally I saw religion as the key to a sound public morality and that in turn as the basis of a sound political order. I came to abandon that view as wishful thinking.

Morality in any context must grow from realistic moral experience of the effects that patterns of cooperation can have on people's well-being, their dignity, and the quality of their relationships. Sound decision procedures cannot guarantee sound moral perceptions, but they are a necessary condition of the shared experience from which alone moral awareness can grow once we go beyond face-to-face relationships.

I addressed the task of showing how this conception might be elaborated to meet different problems from the very local to the international in scale and complexity. I tried to anticipate objections and speculate on its benefits. I was well aware it would not work in all cultural contexts. It was not hard to imagine societies where there was an assumption that only senior males should be chosen as representatives or where the rotation of offices was a matter of taking turns at the trough. My presentation was inevitably utopian inasmuch as there are no existing models of such a system and no reason for thinking that existing institutions and practices would evolve in that direction. I was not a political activist and I had no concrete proposals concerning ways in which these procedures might be introduced in particular circumstances.

I set out my proposals in a book: *Is Democracy Possible?* Published in 1985 by Polity Press, Oxford and University of California Press, Berkeley, it went through two printings. It was translated into German as *Uber Democratie: Alternativen zum Parliamentarismus* and published by Wagenbach, Berlin, 1987. It was republished with a new foreword by Sydney University Press in 2008, as well as on the website setis.library.usyd.edu.au/democracy. To describe my proposals I appropriated the word 'demarchy' from FA Hayek, whose criticisms of current democracies influenced me, but whose suggestions for reform hardly amounted to a distinct conception of politics. I was also associated with an international group of scholars interested in statistical representation who called themselves 'kleroterians'.

What I hoped to achieve was to stimulate discussion, turning political philosophers away from exclusive concentration on the justification, role and limits of state power to consider other kinds of authorities and the whole range of problems concerning the provision of public goods. It did not take off. Philosophers found it too much a matter of empirical speculation rather than conceptual analysis, while political scientists were uninterested in the absence of empirical instances to study. Most of those who were interested came from outside these disciplines.

My thought had developed out of critical reflection on Marxism and capitalism and my experience with participatory democracy in the seventies, which led me to ask whether disciplined, constructive and responsible participatory democratic procedures were possible. One hope that I entertained was that when some Communist Luther rejected authoritarianism and sought to give substance to the label 'People's Democracies', he might find my ideas useful. So I was delighted when in 1989 I received a letter, posted in Norway, from a youth league organiser in Murmansk who had read my book in the Lenin Library in Moscow and proposed to translate it into Russian. A couple of years later he wrote to say the translation was finished, but in the new Russia no publisher was interested in political philosophy, only in quick-selling trash. This hope finally resurfaced in regard to China. In 2006 the government of the small province of Zeguo, influenced by James Fishkin, an American advocate of 'deliberative democracy', set up a statistically chosen committee to decide on its priorities for public works. The key importance of this case is that, in contradistinction to the many other cases of deliberative committees Fishkin and others had sponsored, the government undertook to abide by the committee's decisions, and in fact did so. That makes the crucial difference. The Zeguo experiment has been very successful.[2] It remains to be seen whether the example spreads.

---

2 Obviously it offers a way of introducing democratic participation and minimizing corruption without introducing new political parties that might

I believed that active participation in public affairs was of great importance for the health of society, but that assumption was now regarded as mistaken. The managerial revolution was in full swing. Efficiency and effectiveness in collective action of all sorts depended on firm and decisive management. Participation by clients and decision by committee was a waste of time. Managers should research the preferences of their clients by market survey. It was then up to the clients to accept or reject what management produced, in politics as in commerce. It was assumed that the overriding interests of managers lie in producing what the customers want.

In fact, as we are learning at great cost, any organisation tends to be run in the interests of those who have power in the organisation and their interests are often best served, at least in the short run, by policies that are contrary to the interests of their clients and supporters, as well as to the health of the economy and the body politic. The ways we tried to bring the powerful to account, frequent elections, sensationalised exposure and attention to the bottom line served only to privilege the short term perspective. The worst instances of failure to address this basic problem are at the international level where there are no authorities capable of addressing constructively such problems as climate change and the international monetary system. Any attempt to devise authoritative controls is hostage to the internal politics of nation states in which the actors seek power rather than the good of those on whose behalf they make decisions. Perhaps we may realise before it is too late that the needed authorities must be constituted on a new and independent basis.

---

seem attractive to the Communist Party. On the other hand, it is contrary to the elitist traditions of Chinese culture and the arbitrary powers of its officials. The experiment has attracted attention, even a piece in TIME magazine September 2nd, 2010. See also www.participedia.net/wiki/Wenling_City_Deliberative_Poll and James Fishkin *When the People Speak*, chapter 6.

Prospects of Cooperation

Friendly critics often accused me of having too optimistic a view of human nature or perhaps too narrow a view of its possibilities. It is certainly true that rational cooperation is not the only way of giving meaning to human life. In many cultures, and even in the most highly respected religions, violence has been given ritualised honour and celebrated as noble courage, in contrast to insidious and cowardly evil. In the myth of the warrior violence in the service of the good is wholly admirable. It demonstrates ultimate commitment, putting one's life at risk for the greater good. In its most extreme versions that view amounts to the claim that might is right. In religious doctrines in which the right is constituted by the will of the creator, might manifests that will. It confers his approval, since what emerges is the product of his power. In naturalistic evolutionist doctrines what survives in the struggle for life is the best by definition. The moral absurdity of such doctrines is manifest, but their emotive appeal is undeniable.

More insidious is the view that all societies are vulnerable to violence and that violence can be contained only by the threat of more powerful violence. This is doubly false. On the one hand, as we have learned, the threat of retributive violence is not enough to deter those who seek redemption, glory, revenge or the ultimate good through violence. They find justification in the violence employed against them. Ultimately their violence has to be delegitimised, so that nobody praises, justifies or even condones it. That depends on constructing ways of handling rationally the conflicts that, uncontained, lead to violence. To a great extent containing conflicts is a matter of people learning to agree to differ, to respect the right of others to their own views and activities and to accept that one's own views have the same civil status. That acceptance in turn depends on the existence of effective procedures for reaching practical solutions to those problems that call for collective decision. As long as crude power rules it will be glorified.

On the other hand, delegitimising violence is not enough. There will always also be illegitimate violence wherever there is an opportunity for individuals or groups to advantage themselves thereby. It is true that countering illegitimate violence often involves a measure of violence, but not of greater violence so much as effective mobilisation of all relevant resources, especially protective measures, information and certainty of retribution. While it is true that civil peace has been built on the state's monopoly of legitimate violence, it is not the quantity or quality of the violence the state can unleash that is effective in this respect, but its web of controls that are so difficult to evade. Any complex society is going to need such a web of cooperating and mutually supporting controls, using force as a last resort, but it does not need leviathan, or even centralisation of ultimate power. Power of decision on every question must stop somewhere. But there does not need to be a single authority which has the ultimate decision on all questions. All that is required is agreement about which authority decides which questions.

Evil is defeated, not by violence, but by constructing good institutions and practices based on sound analyses of what is possible, what nourishes a rich variety of creative meaningful activities in which the most diverse talents can flourish. There is a tendency, common to both radical and reactionary ideologies, encouraged by exclusive religions, to think that community depends on singleness of purpose, a shared vision to which all members of the community are dedicated. That is true, up to a point. The crucial limitation is that the tighter the bonds that bind members of a community together, the greater the range of possibilities it excludes. It develops its own rules, icons, rituals and affective style, which some find intensely satisfying. Others, however, not only fail to respond to it, but find its claiming authority over them oppressive and spurious. Many religious congregations that have built up a strong community lose the participation of many who find the pressures to conform increasingly uncongenial and its ethos sanctimonious. Sects are strong on community, but notoriously fissiparous and friable. Social and political movements sustain a sense of community as long as their focus is a clear adversary or a concrete objective. When they attempt to articulate more positive goals they lose cohesion. Opinions differ, not just about the relative importance of conflicting goals or about tactics, strategies and alliances, but about the emotional commitments that community feeling demands. Many independent women deny they are feminists, conservationists deny they are greenies, and so on.

My conclusion was that this was not something to be deplored. It was the dynamics of the search for identity. That search could never be completed, because, far from converging on a single all-embracing realisation of what it is to be human, it produced increasingly diverse and specialised ways of living, all of which displayed in some degree the ways in which we might find fulfilment. Most individuals found themselves relating in ever changing ways, sometimes enthusiastically, sometimes with hostility, often with merely speculative interest, to different spheres of activity, different ways of dealing with life's problems and different ambitions. Out of the chaotic mix of differences new identities, new problems and new approaches to old problems continually emerged. That fluidity bred uncertainty and insecurity. But for most of us most of the time the rich possibilities that it offered were ample compensation.

I found the history of the arts a powerful confirmation of this conclusion. In most cultures the styles, themes and idioms of the various arts had changed frequently over time. Foreign influences were absorbed, changes in technology exploited, traditional beliefs, hopes and fears reinterpreted and older forms of expression exhausted. It is the distinctive and almost certainly irreversible achievement of contemporary culture to see in the variety of past and present works of art not a host of failures but an inexhaustible deposit of specific successes from which we can learn. In some respects this makes our situation more difficult. We can no longer make music with the confidence Bach displayed in expressing the religious sensibility of his age. Whatever we do betrays the consciousness of its historical limitations and its partiality even in relation to its immediate context. The more powerful its idiom the more specific is the range of what it can express. It is just that particularity that makes progress possible, openness to the new a necessity and diversity a matter for rejoicing.

In the light of this vision the basis of cooperation is often not agreement about shared goals but preparedness to help each other attain our own particular goals. The point of political activity is not to construct social unanimity, but to find ways of handling constructively the enormous range of divergent interests that arise from the complexity and volatility of our civilisation.

Democratic Excellence

Nietzsche attacked morality as the means by which the weak and mean constrained the nobly strong. Democracy meant the rule of the weak and base, dragging down the aristocratic ideal of the great and the good. Many different people have felt the force of his critique, and reaction against the many depressing features of mass democracy, coupled with mass consumerism, reinforces its appeal. Envy, resentment and levelling down are enemies of excellence and of freedom. The solution is not to exalt the power of a few who can set higher standards because they refuse to bow to conventional restraints, but to initiate a process in which higher standards are continually being set in the effort to get beyond the limits of the given, not for the sake of being different, but in the search for solutions to the problems that emerge from the process of problem solving itself.

Great achievements in the sciences and the arts are rightly associated with the innovating vision of rare individuals, but work of those individuals springs from and must be accepted within the relevant community of those interested. The community sustains the matrix of social practices and concerns that supply the criteria by which innovative contributions are assessed. Their being accepted and understood, their social authority, depends entirely on there being communities that are capable of incorporating the new into their traditions. Creative individuals are likely to emerge and flourish only when the pursuit of excellence of a particular kind is deeply entrenched in a community specially devoted to doing what needs to be done as well as it possibly can and to judging contributions to that task on their merits.

It is the homogenised mass character of democracy, sustained by centralised power, not grassroots participation, that is the enemy of excellence. Similar considerations apply to consumerism. Part of the answer to the problems of consumerism consists in a shift of focus from the satisfactions of conspicuous consumption to those of contributing to and identifying with excellence in collective achievements. People not only can identify with communities. They need to do so, to prize as their own the triumphs of teams, enterprises and communities they support. In a free community we construct identities for ourselves by choosing the specific communities of interest with which we bond. The more substance and recognition that is given to such bonds the more valued they may be expected to become in comparison with the mere possession of items of consumption. In a participatory culture it is to be expected that people will be accorded status and worth primarily on the value of their contributions to valued achievements. Whether that is a sufficient answer to the problems of consumerism in a society where most goods and services are produced by market capitalism remains to be seen.

Consumerism is only one of its problems to which I had no firm answer. I suggested that the finance for public goods might be derived from vesting natural resources in public bodies which would charge high prices for the use of them with a view to ecological considerations and to providing funds for public goods. In the face of a global pressure on non-renewable resources, it seems certain that the rents derived from the ownership of them are going to rise in any case. In the context of the ecological necessity to manage our consumption of them on a global scale and in a long-term perspective, it seems absurd to leave the use of natural resources to the kind of short-term monetary considerations that govern the market.

However, even if suitably decentralised public ownership of natural resources were instituted, that would still leave capitalism substantially untouched as our way of catering for private consumption. If the various critics of capitalism are right, the reforms I suggest may not be radical enough. We cannot know. It is extremely dangerous to think that there is just one set of practices that is appropriate to handling all problems. They all are appropriate only to a certain kind of problems, are subject to preconditions of many different kinds and work well only on a certain scale. My central conviction is that we must get away from the situation where we are caught between the Scylla of state control and the Charybdis of capitalism as the only means of handling problems of production. It is not a question of looking for panaceas, but of solutions that are appropriate in specific contexts.

The difficulty that is most commonly urged against calls for specialised decentralised authorities is that there is no adequate basis for their authority. Authority may need legitimacy, but it also needs power to enforce its decisions. At least in short-term practical matters, enforcement seems inevitably to be a matter of force, ultimately the state's monopoly of legitimate violence. I do not think this is true. Already there are numerous authorities in religion, sport, the professions, science and even business which have very considerable authority and adequate sanctions to force individuals to obey them in most cases, without relying on any specific legal authorisation, much less any appeal to violence. Even many international bodies that were set up by agreements among states often evolve so as to enjoy authority in their own right. Bodies such as those that set standards for aviation or shipping, various health and ecological organisations exercise unchallenged authority in their specific jurisdictions even over state authorities. In practice authorities depend ultimately on recognition, especially recognition by those other authorities with which they interact. A network of authorities need not derive from a single overriding source. Recognised authorities can support each other by invoking sanctions against offenders. Appreciating the possibilities this opens up is one more instance of the importance of getting beyond the foundationalist mindset in theory and practice.

At a more speculative level, I thought that there was a profound connection between theist ways of thinking and traditional political thinking. The whole of creation depended on the will of God. In tracing all design back to his decision we were supposed to reach the basis of all true understanding. In submitting to his will we achieved our destiny as his creatures. Similarly ultimate political authority was supposed to repose in the sovereign, to whose decisions all good results were attributable and to whom his subjects owed ultimate obedience. The earthly fulfilment of the subject lay in identification with the power of the monarch, or the nation conceived as a sovereign entity. Not so long ago we all sang:

> Land of Hope and Glory, Mother of the free, How shall we repay
> thee, We who were born of thee?
> Wider still and wider, May thy bounds be set. God who made
> thee mighty,
> Make thee mightier yet.

Even in its democratic forms this sort of worship of the sovereign persisted. In going to war to preserve the Union, Lincoln believed that unless it could show itself capable of maintaining its sovereign power, democracy would perish. A nation that could not vindicate its authority by war could neither hold its place among the nation states nor continue to command the loyalty of its citizens. Eighty years later a variant of the same belief, bolstered by a racist conception of the nation, was to lead to the replacement of the Weimar Republic by the Third Reich and to some of the worst atrocities in human history. Nations everywhere have struggled, with disastrous results, to assert their unity, sovereignty and independence, to stamp out dissent and ultimately to mobilise compulsorily all their citizens and all their resources to fight to the death to preserve or extend that sovereignty.

The view that order and design can exist only as the product of an all-powerful designer has been discredited in the case of order in nature by Darwinian forms of explanation and in economic, social and intellectual matters by an understanding of markets, of social processes and of theoretical inquiry. The remaining task is to show in practice how appropriate collective decisions may be derived by a process of negotiation within and between bodies in which diverse interests are negotiated, starting with particular problems in specific contexts.

Later Years

In 1990 the university offered substantial inducements to early retirement to those who had more than two years of tenure left. Having little more than two years left before mandatory retirement, I accepted the offer. Margaret had at least seventeen more years left on her contract and was just entering the full flowering of her career. I needed an occupation. One thing I knew a good deal about was sailing boats. So I bought a small yacht brokerage, idyllically located on one of the most beautiful bays of Middle Harbour. Dashing around the harbour showing yachts to people was a very attractive lifestyle. Naturally, it attracted a lot more hopefuls than the market could support. Soon after I bought into it interest rates soared to 18% and the market for even the modest yachts in which the brokerage specialised collapsed. I hung on for a couple of years, losing money in the process. The world of business was not for me. I retired to a life of modest voluntary activities on behalf of various causes and reading.

About this time, too, my tinnitus became more severe and more persistent and my hearing deteriorated dramatically. I could not follow a lecture or participate in a seminar or even communicate successfully by telephone. Meeting with old friends one on one was the only social activity that I could conduct successfully. But I was highly self-sufficient, interested in books of every sort and films with subtitles, though music became increasingly unpleasant with hearing aids and inaudible without them. I continued to reflect on the problems of philosophy and of every aspect of human life, but was not much inclined to put my thoughts on paper, mainly because I thought I had little that was genuinely original to say about most topics that interested me. Still I was very happy with the outcomes of my own life, especially within the family, and was encouraged by the many changes for the better that I had seen in my lifetime to hope that one day a solution, if not my solution, would emerge to the problems I had identified in the crucial area of the provision of public goods.

An area that I felt needed rethinking in the light of my political and moral concerns is the rule of law. At a very general level the same problems that affect bureaucracy affect law. On the one hand, the demand that anybody subject to a legal restriction should be able to know in advance what is forbidden requires that the law should be as simple as possible. On the other hand, fairness to different people in different circumstances requires that the law take account of relevant differences. The general tendency of legislation in modern times has been towards attempting to increase substantive fairness at the expense of increased complications. That in turn increases the role of lawyers and popular dissatisfaction with the unpredictability of the outcomes of litigation. One function of legal processes is to divert demands for the righting of wrongs and the punishment of offenders away from uncontrolled private retribution towards a rational and principled process that is socially desirable and sustainable. If it is to succeed in this aim, the legal system needs both to educate public opinion about its problems and to find ways of assuring that its outcomes are fair. I believe that citizen committees producing recommendations for legislation can help in the education process and that a review of the jury system to make jury service less burdensome and more satisfactory is needed.

More fundamentally, there are many problems that legal processes cannot handle satisfactorily, and facing up to these problems would, I believe, lead us towards substituting other procedures instead of law in many of the roles law now plays in social life. The obvious examples are the criminalisation of activities that are certainly socially harmful in their systemic effects, but in the short term and in the particular instance involve only a risk of harm to the individual. Drug taking and some kinds of commercial practices are cases in point. Where there is no direct harm to other individuals, social pressure, education and assistance in coping with temptations are likely to be more effective in reducing undesirable behaviour than fining or imprisonment. But these things require organisation and the participation of capable people who are well rewarded and not too constrained by bureaucracy. It is a lot to ask. Legislating prohibitions seems so much easier.

I did try to intervene in an instance where the incapacity of legal procedures to deal with a problem led to what I thought was a very dangerous attempt to give unfettered power to bureaucrats. The 1998 act to introduce the goods and services tax provided that in issuing declarations of liability for unpaid tax the commissioner of taxation might 'treat as having happened something that did not actually happen' or 'treat as not having happened something that did actually happen'. The point was that while it was not too difficult to prove that somebody had not been paying tax, it was often impossible to establish just how much was owing and consequently what the penalty should be. So the taxation department was given the power to make it up, without any recourse for the accused. I mounted a campaign to have some independent review procedure established. I wrote to politicians, newspapers, retired judges, legal academics, accountants and others, largely without success, except for the chartered accountants, who undertook to raise the matter with the department. Nothing happened, in spite of the power being so obviously open to abuse and corruption. People had no sympathy with tax evaders, but in fact what was behind the refusal of recourse was just the convenience of the bureaucrats.

A similar situation later arose in response to terrorism. Legal retribution is retrospective, punishing crimes already committed. It does not deter the terrorist. Prevention of harm seems to require pre-emptive action against those suspected of planning terrorist attacks, including detention on mere suspicion and 'enhanced interrogation' to extract information. Again, any sort of independent review was rejected, though abuses of these powers were well documented. Security of information was more important than the rights of people who might be innocent of any intention to do harm. Neither general considerations about the effects of a practice nor considerations of consistency or justice had much sway against the desire of the various security agencies to have a free hand. Again new kinds of review of their actions seem necessary.

Envoi

Looking back on my quest for a unassailable and potent answer to the meaning of life and the real remedy for the ills of the world, I was not disappointed by my failure to find any comprehensive and irrefutable answer to the questions with which I began. There is no such thing as *the* meaning of life and no right answer to the problems of the world, but many answers that are inevitably partial and provisional in one or more of the various ways in which they need to be assessed. Some of these I have tried to illustrate from my own experience. The great lesson I draw from that experience is the positive appreciation that there are many activities and relationships in life that are full of meaning and there is no end to the ways in which we can continue to refine, enrich and appreciate those meanings. To repeat: What matters is not what we are made of, but what we can make of what we are made of. Grasping that point is the fundamental challenge of our age.

Discovery of ourselves is not a matter of finding some preset plan or list of directions, but of reproducing what needs to be preserved of our natural and constructed heritage and of inventing relationships, enactments and practices that go beyond our present capacities in ways that we can sustain and reflectively endorse.

Socrates concentrated on asking questions rather than announcing answers, but on one topic he delivered a strong verdict: An unexamined life is not worth living.

He was wrong. It is not true that an unexamined life is never worth living. Given a bit of luck in the genetic lottery and favourable circumstances, extroverts can do and die as heroes, untroubled by a hint of self-doubt. Their spontaneity can be very attractive. Even the most reflective find it enviable.

Moreover, if an unexamined life is no good in the first place, examining it is not going to make it any better. Mulling over it will only make it worse.

That is surely right if one examines one's life from the outside, as one might examine a candidate for a position or as a judge might apply the law, even a divinely sanctioned law.

What Socrates wanted to recommend is a way of life in which critical reflection on one's beliefs and desires is a central and valued part of living, constantly modifying one's hopes and strivings in the light of one's own values.

Of course, one still needs quite a bit of luck, though probably not as much as an unreflective person. I have been lucky.

Acknowledgments

I am very conscious of having been supported throughout my life by the contributions, whether voluntary or involuntary, of my parents, of the Catholic community and of Australian taxpayers, many of whom would not approve of the use I have made of the opportunities I have been given. I can only hope that some good may come from my attempts to discharge my obligations to them.

Many of my friends have encouraged and assisted me in writing this text as it progressed through numerous drafts. My poor memory cannot possibly retrieve all of their contributions. Paul Crittenden showed me where an early draft needed a lot of work. Rowanne Couch cast an experienced editorial eye over a later draft from a non-philosopher's perspective, as did Jenny Gribble and Gretchen Poiner. Genevieve Lloyd, Keith Campbell, Gyorgy Markus and Graeme de Graaff made helpful comments, especially on philosophical matters, and encouraged me to persevere. Edmund Campion looked kindly on it from an historian's perspective. Creagh Cole read several drafts, including the penultimate one, with minute and constructive attention to detail. Malcolm Campbell, a physicist and old sparring partner, also commented on the text in some detail.

Margaret Harris has watched over the evolution of the text with close reading and sympathy, bringing to bear on it her incomparable experience as a critic and editor of texts. David Malouf made an exception to his long-established rule when he agreed to launch the book. Susan Murray-Smith and Agata Mrva-Montoya at Sydney University Press have provided very sympathetic support.

Of course, none of these friends share all my opinions. They have, nevertheless, tried generously to help me express them. If the results are half-baked, it is because I kept fiddling with the oven.

Books Mentioned in the Text

Anscombe, Elizabeth (1957). *Intention*. Oxford: Blackwell.

Bachelard, Gaston (1964). *The Psychoanalysis of Fire*. London: Routledge & Kegan Paul.

Bachelard, Gaston (1964). *The Poetics of Space*. New York: Orion Press.

Belloc, Hilaire (1912). *The Servile State*. London: Foulis.

Belloc, Hilaire (1932). *An Heroic Poem in Praise of Wine*. Plaistow, Newham: Curwen Press.

Burnheim, John (2006 [1985]). *Is Democracy Possible? The Alternative to Electoral Democracy*. Sydney: Sydney University Press.

Crittenden, Paul (2008). *Changing Orders: Scenes of Clerical and Academic Life*. Blackheath, NSW: Brandl & Schlesinger.

Dondeyne, Albert (1963 [1958]). *Contemporary European Thought and Christian Faith*. Pittsburgh, PA: Duquesne University Press.

Fishkin, James S (2009). When the People Speak: Deliberative Democracy and Public Consultation. Oxford, New York: Oxford University Press.

Geraghty, Christopher (2003). *The Priest Factory: A Manly Vision of Triumph 1958–1962 and Beyond*. Melbourne: Spectrum Publications.

Geraghty, Christopher (2001). *Cassocks in the Wilderness: Remembering the Seminary at Springwood*. Richmond, Vic.: Spectrum Publications.

Hayek, Friedrich August von (1944). *The Road to Serfdom. London:* Routledge Press.

Johnson, Dean Hewlett (1939). *The Socialist Sixth of the World.* London: Victor Gollancz Ltd.

Keneally, Thomas (1964). *The Place at Whitton.* London: Cassell.

Keneally, Thomas (1968). *Three Cheers for the Paraclete.* Sydney: Angus and Robertson.

Marks, Karl (1976–81 [1867]). *Capital: A Critique of Political Economy.* Harmondsworth: Penguin.

Orwell, George (1949). *Nineteen Eighty-Four.* London: Secker and Warburg.

Roberts, Stephen (1938). *The House that Hitler Built.* London: Methuen.

Russell, Bertrand (1948). *Human Knowledge, Its Scope and Limits.* New York: Simon and Schuster.

Sheehan, Michael (1950 [1923] *Apologetics and Catholic Doctrine: A Two Years' Course of Religious Instruction for Schools and Colleges,* 4th edn. Dublin: MH Gill.

Smith, Adam (2002 [1757]). *Theory of Moral Sentiments.* Cambridge: Cambridge University Press.

Whitehead, Alfred North and Bertrand Russell (1927 [1910, 1912, 1913]). *Principia Mathematica,* 3 vols. Cambridge: University Press.

Wittgenstein, Ludwig (1958 [1922]). *Tractatus Logico-Philosophicus,* London: Routledge & Kegan Paul.

Index

A

Made in the USA
Lexington, KY
15 February 2012